Contents

Willy Russell   v

Plot   xi

Commentary   xx
  The context   xx
  Genre   xxxi
  Structure   xxxv
  Rita   xl
  Frank   lii
  The play's reception   lx
  The 2003 revised version   lxvi
  The film version   lxxi

Further Reading   lxxv

Educating the author   lxxix

EDUCATING RITA   1

Notes   83

Questions for Further Study   100

Steve Lewis would like to thank Willy Russell for sharing his thoughts, insights and recollections about the play

Willy Russell

1947   Born William Martin Russell, 23 August, in
       Whiston, a town in Merseyside about eight miles
       east of Liverpool city centre.
1952   Family moves to a rural village in Knowsley on the
       outskirts of Liverpool.
1958   Goes to Woolfall Secondary School, 'a chaotic badly
       run school'.
1959   Moves to a more rural school in Rainford.
1962   Leaves school with one O level. Sits the entry
       examination to become an apprentice printer
       and fails, so signs up to train as hairdresser
       instead.
1963   Works as a ladies' hairdresser in Kirkby, Liverpool.
       Writes stories and songs and performs around clubs
       on the folk music circuit.
1966   Meets his future wife, Ann Seagroatt.
1968   Gives up hairdressing and works as a labourer at the
       Bear Brand warehouse to raise enough money to
       return to education.
1969   Attends Childwall College of Further Education to
       study for O levels. Marriage to Ann Seagroatt.
1970   Trains to become a drama teacher at St Katherine's
       College, Liverpool.
1971   Sees *Unruly Elements* by John McGrath at the
       Everyman Theatre which spurs him on to become
       a playwright. Debut stage play, *Keep Your Eyes
       Down*, performed by students at St Katherine's
       College.
1972   *Blind Scouse* (a triple bill of student productions of the
       plays, *Keep Your Eyes Down*, *Sam O'Shanker* and
       Playground) is performed at the Edinburgh Fringe.
       This production brings Willy Russell to the attention
       of the playwright, John McGrath, who helps secure

him his first professional commission for the
Everyman Theatre in Liverpool.

1973   Obtains his Certificate in Education. Teaches at
Shorefields School in Toxteth. This experience
provides the source material for the later television
plays, *Our Day Out* and *One Summer*. *When the Reds*,
adapted from Alan Plater's *The Tigers Are Coming –
OK*, produced at the Everyman Theatre and
directed by Pam Brighton. *King of the Castle*, a play
for television, screened on BBC2 in November. *Tam
Lin*, a musical play for children, produced at
Dovecot Primary School, for which Willy Russell
wrote the songs as well as the script. *Sam O'Shanker*, a
new musical version of the earlier play, written for
Vanload, the Everyman Theatre's touring company.

1974   *John, Paul, George, Ringo . . . and Bert* opens in May at
the Everyman Theatre, directed by Alan Dosser.
Transfers in August to the Lyric Theatre,
Shaftesbury Avenue, London, winning both the
Evening Standard and London Critics' awards for Best
Musical. A London cast recording with Barbara
Dickson released on RSO records. *Death of a Young
Young Man* fails to win the *Radio Times* TV Drama
competition but is produced and shown in January
1975 as a BBC *Play for Today*. *The Tale of Blind Joey
McSweeney* is Willy Russell's contribution to the
Everyman Theatre's ten-year-anniversary Christmas
show, *The Cantril Tales*. Gives up teaching to become
a full-time writer. Son Robert is born.

1975   *Breezeblock Park*, directed by Alan Dosser at the
Everyman Theatre. Revived in September 1977 at
the Mermaid Theatre, London, transferring to the
Whitehall Theatre in November. The cast includes
Prunella Scales, Julie Walters (the original Rita of
Educating Rita) and Pete Postlethwaite. *Break In*,
written for BBC Schools, is shown in the BBC *Scene*
series.

1976   Writer-in-residence at C.F. Mott College, Liverpool.
One for the Road opens at the Contact Theatre,

Manchester, under the title *Painted Veg and Parkinson*, directed by Caroline Smith. *Our Day Out* is commissioned as a television play by the BBC and broadcast. Its success earns it a repeat showing six weeks later in the *Play for Today* series.

1977   *I Read the News Today* is broadcast in February in the BBC Schools *Listening and Writing* series. To date it is Willy Russell's only play for radio. Fellow in Creative Writing (1977–9) at Manchester Polytechnic. Daughter Ruth is born.

1978   *Stags and Hens* produced at the Liverpool Everyman in October, directed by Chris Bond. *Lies*, a two-part play for the BBC Schools series *Scene*, broadcast in November.

1979   *The Daughters of Albion* produced by Yorkshire Television and shown in May as part of the ITV *Playhouse* series. New version of *One for the Road* opens at Nottingham Playhouse, directed by Mike Ockrent, starring Prunella Scales and Alun Armstrong. *Band on the Run*, a screenplay, written for Paul McCartney Productions with Mike Ockrent but not produced.

1980   *Politics and Terror*, an eight-minute sketch commissioned by Granada Television and shown in the *Celebration* programme in February. *The Boy with the Transistor Radio*, a much re-worked version of Willy Russell's first play *Keep Your Eyes Down*, is produced by Thames Television for the ITV Schools series *The English Programme*. *Educating Rita*, commissioned by the Royal Shakespeare Company, opens at the Warehouse Theatre, Covent Garden, on 10 June, starring Julie Walters and Mark Kingston, directed by Mike Ockrent. The production transfers to the Piccadilly Theatre, London, in September, where it runs for three years. The play wins the Society of West End Theatres award for Best Comedy. Daughter Rachel is born.

1981   *Blood Brothers*, written for Merseyside Young People's Theatre Company as a one-act play, directed by

Paul Harman. The first performance takes place at Fazakerley Comprehensive School in Liverpool in November. Directs a new production of *Educating Rita* for the Liverpool Playhouse. Associate Director of Liverpool Playhouse (1981–3), along with Alan Bleasdale, Chris Bond and Bill Morrison.

1982   Writes the book, music and lyrics of *Blood Brothers*, based on the earlier school version.

1983   The film version of *Educating Rita* is released. The film is produced and directed by Lewis Gilbert and stars Michael Caine and Julie Walters. The screenplay is nominated for an Academy award and wins a BAFTA award for Best Film. *Blood Brothers – the Musical* opens at Liverpool Playhouse in January, starring Barbara Dickson and directed by Chris Bond, and transfers to the Lyric Theatre, Shaftesbury Avenue, London, in April. Awarded an Honorary MA by the Open University. *Our Day Out – the Musical*, Willy Russell's own stage adaptation of the 1977 television play, opens in April at the Liverpool Everyman with songs by Willy Russell, Chris Mellor and Bob Eaton (who also directed the production). *One Summer*, a five-part television serial made by Yorkshire TV for Channel Four, is transmitted in August.

1984   *Blood Brothers*, new touring production, directed by Chris Bond.

1985   Composes the theme song for Ron Hutchinson's television series *Connie*.

1986   Composes the music for the film, *Mr Love*, written by Ken Eastaugh and directed by Roy Battersby. *Shirley Valentine* opens at the Liverpool Everyman in March, directed by Glen Walford and starring Noreen Kershaw.

1987   *One for the Road*, a new production starring Russ Abbott, at the Lyric Theatre, Shaftesbury Avenue.

1988   *Shirley Valentine* opens in a new production at the Vaudeville Theatre, London, starring Pauline Collins and directed by Simon Callow, winning the

Olivier award for Best Comedy. This production transfers to the Booth Theatre, New York, and is nominated for a Tony award for Best Play. *Blood Brothers*, a new production directed by Bob Thomson and Bill Kenwright, opens at the Albery Theatre, London. To date, this production is still running in London's West End.

1989   The film version of *Shirley Valentine*, directed by Lewis Gilbert and starring Pauline Collins, is released.

1990   Writes music and screenplay for film version of *Stags and Hens, Dancin' Thru' the Dark* directed by Mike Ockrent.

1992   Awarded an Honorary D.Lit. by the University of Liverpool. Writes a new text for Stravinsky's *The Soldier's Tale* and takes the role of the Narrator.

1993   *Terraces*, originally written for BBC Schools Television and published in 1973, is eventually shown in January. *Blood Brothers – the Musical* opens at the Music Box Theatre, New York, in April and runs for two years.

1995   Willy Russell is made a Fellow of John Moores University. Performs in an evening of prose, poetry, song and music, *Words on the Run*, with poets Adrian Henri, Brian Patten, Roger McGough and musician Andy Roberts. The show tours festivals in 1996 and again in 1997.

1996   *Our Day Out*, a much revised version of the earlier musical, staged at the Belgrade Theatre, Coventry.

2000   *The Wrong Boy*, his first novel, published – the story of Raymond Marks, a shy misunderstood teenager, told in the form of letters written to the singer/song-writer Morrissey in June 1991.

2002   *Educating Rita*, a new production using a revised version of the text, is staged at the Liverpool Playhouse, directed by Glen Walford with Angela Clarke as Rita and Richard O'Callaghan as Frank.

2003   Records and releases an album of his own songs, *Hoovering the Moon*.

2004   *In Other Words*, a touring show of music, songs, verse
and readings performed by Willy Russell and Tim
Firth. The Willy Russell Foundation Award is
established to promote new writing at the
Edinburgh International Festival.

2006   *Educating Rita*, a production set in modern-day
Cardiff, opens at the Sherman Theatre, Cardiff,
directed by Phil Clark and starring Ruth Jones and
Steve Speirs. Writes screenplay for the musical,
Blood Brothers.

Plot

Act One

Scene One

Frank, a university lecturer in English Literature in his early fifties, is surveying the bookshelves of his study in search of something. He eventually finds a bottle of whisky behind several volumes of novels by Charles Dickens and pours the last few inches into a mug. Frank answers the telephone and it becomes apparent that he is expected home for dinner by his partner, Julia. However, he tells her that he is working late because he is waiting for his first Open University student to arrive. There is repeated knocking at the door: the person outside is having difficulty opening it. Frank puts down the phone and Rita, a woman in her mid-twenties, enters complaining about the state of the door handle.

While Frank is looking for his paperwork, Rita's attention alights on a print of naked figures in a religious scene and their first discussion surrounds the distinction between the picture as a work of religious art and medieval pornography. Rita says she is surprised that she was accepted as a student and Frank admits that she represents his first experience of teaching for the Open University. They begin to get the measure of each other by teasing. Frank declines Rita's offer of a cigarette as he has recently given up. This leads to a discussion about fighting death and the relative merits of Dylan Thomas's and Roger McGough's poetic treatment of the subject.

Frank offers Rita a drink, which he finds behind a copy of E. M. Forster's *Howards End*. Rita is surprised to see Frank's secret store of whisky bottles but she reserves her judgement (for now). After some jokes at E.M. Forster's expense, Frank lends Rita *Howards End* to read. Rita gives Frank her views on the difference between the 'properly educated' and 'the masses' and she mentions that she is a hairdresser. Once she establishes that Frank does not object to her swearing, Rita tells him that she has decided to stay. The first literary question Rita asks Frank is for a definition of the term 'assonance' which, from his explanation, she sums up as 'gettin' the rhyme wrong'.

Frank has Rita down on his list as 'Mrs S. White' but when he asks her for her Christian name she says she calls herself Rita after the novelist Rita Mae Brown who wrote *Rubyfruit Jungle*. Frank has never heard of the writer or the novel so Rita lends him her copy. Rita asks Frank his name and in turn he wants to know what she is like as a hairdresser. She says that people go to the hairdresser's hoping to change themselves but she feels you need to change from the inside and she is looking to the course and to Frank to help her do that. Frank finds himself looking at Rita and saying that he thinks she is 'rather marvellous', a compliment she finds hard to take.

Frank wants to know why she has decided to take the course now and Rita explains that she wants more out of life than just to have a baby. It is clear that she is out of step with what her husband wants and what the people around her expect and that she needs to 'find herself'. Frank has another drink and when Rita asks him when he is going to start teaching her, he declares that he is 'an appalling teacher', that she deserves better and that he has decided not to continue with Open University teaching. Rita collects her things and leaves the room only suddenly to decide to return but she is hindered by the broken door handle. She shouts through the door for Frank to let her back in but he tells her to go away. Rita manages to open the door and, despite Frank's decision not to teach her, she tells him that she will be back next week and threatens that she is going to give him a haircut.

Scene Two
Frank is waiting for Rita to arrive and is tempted to get himself a drink when he hears the door handle being fiddled

with from the outside. He goes to the door and finds Rita squirting oil into the handle from an oil can which she gives him to keep. Rita walks in and says she loves Frank's room. She imagines what it must be like to be educated at a private school and compares it with the working-class education she had. Rita describes the low expectations of those around her and how for her a university education means being able to escape.

The lesson begins and Frank gives Rita his feedback on her critical appreciation of *Rubyfruit Jungle*. He explains that her approach is too subjective and she has got to learn to be more analytical and objective in her appreciation of literature. Rita's response to *Howards End* is to say it is 'crap'. Frank points out that unless Rita is prepared to discuss literature more academically she will not pass the exams. Rita changes the subject by asking Frank if he is married. Frank explains that his marriage broke up over poetry. The romantic relationship he had with his wife had been the inspiration for his poetry but his writing became as stagnant as his marriage. Rita wants to buy one of Frank's poetry books but they are long out of print. Frank reveals that he lives with Julia who is one of his ex-students and now a tutor at the university. Rita complains that teachers kill their students' interest by turning it into a lesson. Frank says he would rather run off with Rita than be teaching her and loses his temper with her when she still refuses to take *Howards End* seriously. This turns Rita's attention back to E.M. Forster.

Scene Three

Frank is at his desk with Rita's essay on *Peer Gynt*. Rita is late and hurries in talking non-stop about her day at the hairdresser's. Frank turns straight away to Rita's essay and says that her response to solving the staging difficulties of Ibsen's play with one line, 'doing it on the radio', is not good enough as an essay answer. Frank tries to explain the rules of writing an essay and Rita eventually settles down to re-writing her essay. It is not too long before Rita is talking to Frank again, saying that *Peer Gynt* is about someone in search for the meaning of life. Frank is powerless to stop Rita telling him how she has explained the meaning of *Peer Gynt* to one of her hairdressing clients. This leads her into wanting to discuss the meaning of culture and she describes those from her own background as playing the 'Got-to-Have game'. Frank suggests that she should go into politics but Rita sees gaining an understanding of literature as giving her strength. Rita comments on how her husband, Denny, is frightened by the changes he is seeing in her.

Frank uses the way in which Rita has been making the connections between the things that surround her as a teaching point to explain Forster's use of 'only connect' in *Howards End*. Rita finishes her revised attempt at the *Peer Gynt* essay and Frank reads out her very brief justification for why it should be done on the radio.

Scene Four

Frank wants to know where Rita's essay is and is getting annoyed with her lack of preparation for his tutorials. Rita explains that Denny has discovered that she is still taking the contraceptive pill when he thought they were trying to have a baby. In his anger, Denny has burnt her essay on Chekhov and her books and she cannot understand his objection to her studying. Frank suggests that perhaps Denny thinks she is having an affair with him, but Rita makes it clear that she sees Frank as nothing more than her teacher.

Rita knows that Denny is 'wondering where the girl he married has gone to', but when Frank says that she might think about giving up the course, she compares it to giving up life itself. Rita changes the subject back to Chekhov and wants to know why he is called a 'comic genius' when the events in *The Seagull* are so tragic. Frank explains the nature of 'Chekhovian comedy' and asks Rita if she has ever been to the theatre. Rita admits that she hasn't and suggests they go and see a production of *The Importance of Being Earnest* that she has seen advertised. Frank is reluctant to go because it is an amateur production but he is made to reflect when Rita calls him 'an awful snob'.

Scene Five

Rita turns up unexpectedly at Frank's study during her lunch break. She is bursting to tell someone about a professional production of *Macbeth* she has been to see. Frank is honoured that she has chosen him to share her excitement. When Rita says that she needs to get back to work to prevent a tragedy, Frank uses the opportunity to explain the difference between tragedy in drama and the tragic in real life. Rita invites Frank to go to an art gallery with her the next day and Frank invites her and Denny to have dinner at his house the following Saturday.

Scene Six

Frank is annoyed that Rita did not come to his dinner party and apologised by pushing a note, written on the back of her essay, through his letter box saying, 'Sorry couldn't come'. Rita tells Frank about the big fight she had over it with Denny but says that she was still intending to go on her own. She spent ages looking for the right dress to wear and was afraid of choosing the wrong wine. She felt that she would not be able to say the right things. Frank is furious that Rita should think that he invited her for any reason other than to be herself. This leads Rita into describing how she feels like a freak who no longer belongs to the working-class world she was brought up in nor does she have the confidence yet to be part of the educated class to which she aspires. She tells Frank about her mother crying in the pub because they could have been singing better songs and this has made Rita even more determined to continue with her studies.

Scene Seven

Frank is marking papers when Rita arrives with a holdall. Frank discovers that Denny has told Rita that she either gives up the course or she can pack her bags. Rita has chosen the latter option and is going to stay with her mother until she finds a flat of her own. Frank tries to comfort her but Rita asks for feedback on her *Macbeth* essay. Frank says that the essay is not rubbish but that it is too personalised to pass the examination. Frank is afraid that if he teaches Rita how to write essays just to pass the examination that she will lose her 'uniqueness'. Rita remains determined and, once Frank tells her that she is good enough to do the course, she decides to do whatever it takes to be successful.

Act Two

Scene One

Rita returns from her summer school in London. She relates some of her exploits and tells Frank how she had the confidence to stand up and ask a question about Chekhov in front of two thousand other students. Frank tells her that Julia left him during their holiday in France over an argument about eggs but that they are now back together.

Rita is now living in a flat with Trish and she describes her as someone like Frank in that 'she's got taste'. Rita has brought Frank a present, a pen inscribed 'Must only be used for poetry. By strictest order – Rita'. Rita suggests having their tutorial on the lawn outside but Frank refuses to go. Rita is concerned about Frank's continuing drinking habit but he reminds her that she will not be his student for ever and that she will be leaving him soon.

At Rita's request, Frank finds 'a dead good poet' to teach her but she has already covered the work of William Blake through a lecturer she met at the summer school. Frank is noticeably put out.

Scene Two

Rita arrives late and is talking with a posh accent. Frank
gets her to talk normally and points out that she has grass on
her back. Rita is late because she got into a discussion with
some other students on the relative merits of D. H.
Lawrence's *Lady Chatterley's Lover* and *Sons and Lovers*. Rita has
so impressed the 'proper students' that she has been asked
by Tiger (real name – Tyson) to join them in France for
Christmas. Frank's jealously is apparent when he says, 'Is
there much point in working towards an examination if
you're going to fall in love?' Rita puts him straight about her
relationship with Tiger and wants to know what her latest
essay is like. She is pleased to hear that it is on a par with
the work of Frank's other students.

Scene Three

Rita is already in the room when Frank arrives in a drunken
state. He is swearing and cursing because some of his
students have complained about him being drunk during a
lecture. Rita points out that he is not in a fit state to give her
a tutorial but he sits her down and wants to talk to her about
her essay on Blake's 'The Blossom'. Frank does not like
Rita's rather fashionable interpretation of the poem which
reflects her new friends', but, when she challenges his
criticism of her work, he has to admit that it would get her a
good mark. Frank warns her to be careful about her new-
found independence and Rita makes it clear to him that she
has changed and is different from the woman who first
walked into his study.

Scene Four

Rita is very late for her tutorial and suggests cancelling it.
Frank phoned her at work to find out where she was and
has discovered that she is no longer a hairdresser. Rita
cannot understand why he is making such a fuss over her
changing her job but Frank is obviously annoyed that she

enjoys the company of other students, especially Tiger, more than his these days. Rita wishes he would give up the drink so that they could talk about things that matter. As a challenge, Frank gives Rita copies of his own poetry and asks for a critical essay on them by the following week.

Scene Five

Rita turns up unexpectedly and enthuses about Frank's poetry, using the pretentious language of her new friends. Frank believes that in Rita he has created a monster who can now appreciate literature critically but that the 'old Rita' would have recognised his poetry for the worthless crap it is. Rita turns on him and calls him, 'Mr Self-Pitying Piss-Artist' who cannot bear to see her grow up and think for herself. In her anger, Rita reveals that Frank is the only person who still calls her by the invented name of Rita.

Scene Six

Frank is trying to contact Rita by telephone. He first tries the bistro where she works and then manages to get hold of her flatmate, Trish. He leaves a message to say that he has entered Rita for her examination.

Scene Seven

Rita has brought Frank a Christmas card. She is about to leave when Frank appears with packing cases. His drunkenness has caused the university some embarrassment and he is being sent to Australia for two years. Julia is not going with him. Rita thanks Frank for entering her for the exam and for being a good teacher. She mentions that her flatmate, Trish, who she thought was so together, has tried to kill herself. The first question on the exam was the one Frank had set her about *Peer Gynt* but she chose to answer it the way that an 'educated Rita' would. Frank congratulates her on achieving a good pass and asks her if she would like

to accompany him to Australia. Rita has also got an offer
from Tiger to go to France for Christmas or she might
decide to go to her mother's. She emphasises that the
important thing is that she has a choice and she will make
the decision.

Frank makes Rita a gift of a low-cut dress, the sort of
dress that Rita had promised herself to buy when she was
educated. In return, Rita sits Frank down and starts to give
him the haircut she promised him at the end of her first
lesson.

Commentary

The context

Liverpool is a city which has produced some of the best artistic talent in England. Having been a thriving sea-port on the banks of the River Mersey, it has a history of embracing people from different cultures and countries and this particular mix of languages and people has contributed to its distinctive character. The area has a dialect and language all of its own known as Scouse and anyone from the region is instantly recognisable by the sound of their accent. When the Beatles hit the international stage in the 1960s, Liverpool became associated with a whole genre of popular music known as the Mersey Sound. At the same time a generation of Liverpool poets emerged that included Roger McGough, Brian Patten and Adrian Henri who performed their poetry live and gave poetry a huge popular appeal.

Liverpool is also known for its comedians, such as Ken Dodd, Jimmy Tarbuck and Stan Boardman, and the particular kind of wit associated with Scousers was made popular by the writer Carla Lane in her BBC comedy series *The Liver Birds* and *Bread*. Liverpool also has two producing theatres, the Liverpool Playhouse and the Everyman Theatre. The Playhouse is one of the oldest repertory theatres in the country and associated with traditional work, whereas the Everyman was created in the 1960s and was responsible for developing a particular brand of new work often with a local and political flavour. It is from this background that two of Britain's best-known writers emerged in the 1970s: Alan Bleasdale and Willy Russell. It is a running joke between them that one is often mistaken for the other but their styles and treatment of subject matter are quite different. Bleasdale's work, such as *Boys from the*

Blackstuff, has a darker almost pessimistic side to it whereas there is less of a political edge and a greater degree of optimism in Russell's work. What they have in common is that they write about the place they know and use it as a background to their plays and as an inspiration for their characters and the stories they have to tell.

Willy Russell is one of Britain's most popular playwrights and *Educating Rita* has been in performance somewhere in the world ever since its first appearance on stage in June 1980. The film version, made three years later with Julie Walters and Michael Caine, brought his work to the attention of a much wider public. Even with this kind of success, Willy Russell has remained fiercely loyal to his friends and family on Merseyside, the area of his birth, education and the inspiration for much of his writing. He is a writer from the provinces who has conquered the international stage. His characters and the stories they have to tell have managed to touch audiences all over the world.

In his introduction, 'Educating the author', on page lxxix, Willy Russell provides his own account of how he left school at fifteen and trained as a hairdresser. Like his character Rita, Willy Russell wanted more out of life and gained the required qualifications to train as a teacher by returning to education in his early twenties. The beginnings of *Educating Rita* can be detected in Willy Russell's own memories of studying O-level English Literature at night school when he describes how he wanted to share his excitement for education with his hairdressing customers:

> At nine the next morning I walked in to the shop, a self-appointed expert on the work of George Orwell, with particular reference to *Animal Farm*. As I enthused over the book, my worried and anxious customers exchanged glances of dismay.
>
> 'What's got into him? I think I preferred him when y' couldn't get a bleedin' word out of him.'
>
> 'Pigs! A book about soddin' pigs. He must've been drinkin' perm lotion.'
>
> 'Pigs! He must be thinkin' of goin' into butchery.'

> 'He already has – have y' seen my hair?'
> And so for the best part of a year my long-suffering
> customers had to cope with my conversation and new-found
> beliefs. (Russell in Pye, 1991, p. xi)

Echoes of this 'remembered dialogue' can be heard in the
report Rita gives Frank about the discussion she has had
with one of her customers about *Peer Gynt*. The quick-witted
retort for which Liverpudlians are well known is here in the
comparison between hairdressing and butchery and evident
in the following example where Peer Gynt is thought of as
some sort of hair conditioner:

Rita   I was doin' this woman's hair on Wednesday [. . .] I
was doin' her hair an' I was dead bored with what the others
were talkin' about in the shop so I said to my customer, 'Do
you know about Peer Gynt?' She just thought it was a new
kind of conditioner! So I told her all about it, the play? An' y'
know somethin', she was dead interested.

Frank (*uninterested*)   Was she?

Rita   She said to me this woman, after I'd told her all about
it, she said: 'I wish *I* could go off searchin' for the meanin' of
life. There's loads of them round by us who feel like that.
Because there is no meaning!' (p. 31)

There is a comic dissonance in Rita's final remark with its
sudden change of mood. The reality of life on a council
estate for Rita and her customers is brought into stark
contrast with the poetic philosophising of Ibsen's
protagonist. Peer Gynt's global journey in search of
something better is a world far removed from the down-to-
earth existence of the ordinary people portrayed in Willy
Russell's work. What is evident from Willy Russell's own
upbringing and from the characters and settings in his plays
is his affinity with the working class. The creation of Rita
shows a warmth and truthfulness about the character and
she is never patronised.

By his own admission, Willy Russell writes from his
imagination rather than by making notes and relying on
research, which he sees as getting in the way of the business

of telling the story through his characters. His writing is informed by his experiences and influenced by the unique social conditions and people that living in a city like Liverpool provides. It was a happy coincidence that as he was finding his voice as a playwright, his student work was seen by John McGrath and Alan Dosser, the leading lights of the Liverpool Everyman Theatre. One of the major aims of the Everyman was to create a new type of theatre that would appeal to a broader audience and produce work that was relevant to the people of Liverpool. Willy Russell's first professional work was for the Everyman in 1973. It took the form of a substantial re-working of Alan Plater's *The Tigers Are Coming – OK*, adapted with songs, relocated to Liverpool and re-titled after the Liverpool football club song, *When the Reds*. With this achievement under his belt, Willy Russell was given the chance by Alan Dosser to create a piece about the Beatles which became *John, Paul, George, Ringo . . . and Bert*. After its initial four-week run at the Everyman it transferred to London's West End in August 1974 and ran for over a year, garnering two major awards for best musical. At about the same time, plays written for television started to be accepted and Willy Russell was able to give up his teaching job and become a full-time writer.

Educating Rita was the culmination of an intense period of writing from 1975 to 1980 that included the stage plays *Breezeblock Park* (1975), *One for the Road* (1976), and *Stags and Hens* (1978), and the television play *Our Day Out* (1976) which brought his work to the attention of an even wider audience than his stage plays. All three stage plays received their first productions in the north-west of England but when a revival of *Breezeblock Park* transferred to London's West End in 1977, it was seen by the then literary manager of the Royal Shakespeare Company, Walter Donohue. He admired 'the directness of the play's working-class Christmas setting and the way the traditional "drawing-room" comedy had been turned on its head' (Colin Chambers, programme note for the West End production of *Educating Rita*, 1980). Willy Russell recalls that this transfer of *Breezeblock Park* was something of an unhappy affair and it had a rough ride. Nonetheless, Walter Donohue saw the potential in the play and this led him to commission Willy Russell to write for the Royal Shakespeare Company's experimental studio space in London, the Warehouse (now the Donmar Warehouse). The Warehouse was an apt name for a building that had previously been used as a storehouse by a brewery and its bare brick walls are one of its main features. It is an intimate 250-seater venue that has produced some of the best and most exciting work in London's West End, but Willy Russell's first impression of it was:

> It was all black drapes, Brechtian, experimental, hairshirt theatre. I knew I wanted to put some joy into that place and write something joyous for it. (Interview with Philip Key, 'Educating Rita – and Willy Too', Liverpool Daily Post, 5 April 2002)

Having received this prestigious commission, the next problem was coming up with the right idea to fulfil it. Wanting to bring joy into the Warehouse, one of the early ideas he put to the RSC was a stage adaptation of Our Day Out, which would have required a fairly large cast. However, the resources of the RSC were already heavily committed to their nine-hour and fifty-strong cast version of Dickens's Nicholas Nickleby and Willy Russell was asked to think again. He of course went to the other extreme and limited his resources to two actors and one setting which has made producing Educating Rita a financially attractive proposition ever since.

The origin of Rita can be traced back to characters in earlier Russell plays.

> From Sandra in Breezeblock Park, through Linda in Stags and Hens, through Kathleen [in Daughters of Albion – a television play broadcast in May 1979], I obviously was looking to explore this young woman and it was only when Rita came along that I was able to fully look at this girl. (Russell in Gill, 1992, p. 60)

Breezeblock Park concerns the lives of two related families at Christmas time. Act One of the play is set on Christmas Eve in the home of Syd and Betty and Act Two takes place on Christmas Day at Reeny and Ted's house. The inspiration for the play was reportedly Willy Russell seeing Alan Ayckbourn's *The Norman Conquests* which was playing at the theatre next door to *John, Paul, George, Ringo and . . . Bert* in Shaftesbury Avenue. In place of Ayckbourn's characters from the professional classes and the middle-class setting, Russell's characters are working-class people living on a council estate. Michael Coveney, the theatre critic of the *Financial Times*, went so far as to compare the two playwrights thus: 'I think of his work [WR's] as Alan Ayckbourn with a hairy chest and a hangover' (1980).

Sandra is Betty and Syd's daughter and at nineteen she has decided that she wants to give up work and go to college. Sandra has met Tim, a student, at a party and, rather like Rita, she experiences a world which she associates with culture and a way of life that is better than that lived by her parents. The following conversation Sandra has with her Aunty Vera illustrates how meeting Tim has given Sandra the idea that going to college will enable her to gain entry to a world of 'good taste' and to a class of people that she thinks are better than her own:

Sandra He's different, Aunty Vera. That's all. Look, see – look, his type of life is – different like, like, when I started goin' up to the college with him. You should have seen it, Aunty Vee, honest it just . . . You want to see how they live. It's . . . I went up there one afternoon, and everyone was sittin' round on the lawns, talkin' in the sun. You know, readin' and discussin' things. Honest, everyone was full of life an' interesting. You couldn't believe how people live out there, Aunty Vee. It's just – I mean – all the people he goes round with – they're just so, you know full of life. It made me feel really thick and stupid.

Vera Oh I wouldn't let yourself feel like that, Sandra. They wouldn't make me feel like that.

Sandra An' like Christmas. [. . .] they'll have lots of people round, interesting people, round to dinner. And it'll be a proper dinner, a special dinner, like an event and it'll take hours to get through [. . .] and all the people will sit round the table afterwards and talk and tell stories and laugh. (*Breezeblock Park*, Act One)

The description of students sitting out on the lawn, 'readin' and discussin' things', is an idea that follows through into *Educating Rita*. In the original Act One, Scene One, and in the film version, there is a reference to students studying on the lawn but all that remains of it in the revised version is Rita saying, 'I love that lawn' (p. 19), followed by a comparison with the public schools of Harrow and Eton. This quote from the 1980 version shows how close in character the imagined view of student life is between Sandra and Rita and presumably how it was to some extent for the author returning to education as an adult.

Rita   I love that lawn down there. When it's summer do they sit on it?

Frank (*going to the window*)   Who?

Rita (*going back to the desk*)   The ones who come here all the time. The proper students.

Frank   Yes. First glimmer of sun and they're all out there.

Rita   Readin' an' studyin'?

Frank   Reading and studying? What do you think they are, human? Proper students don't read and study.

Rita   Y'what?

Frank   A joke, a joke. Yes. They read and study, sometimes. (*Educating Rita*, in *Plays: 1*, pp. 295–6)

In the film version, Rita looks out of Frank's study window and says, 'I love that lawn down there with all the proper students.' The play dialogue suggests that the scene is taking place at any time other than during the summer whereas in the film the students are seen sitting on the lawn, the sun is shining and there are leaves on the trees. The difference in the timescale of the play and film will be discussed later.

After her return from summer school and with her renewed confidence, Rita suggests to Frank that they should go outside for their tutorial.

Rita   Come on, let's go an' have the tutorial down there.

Frank (*appalled*)   Down where?

Rita (*getting her bag*)   Down there – on the grass – come on.

Frank   On the grass? Nobody sits out there at this time of year.

Rita   They do – (*Looking out of the window.*) – there's some of them out there now. (p. 58)

This reference to students studying outside on the grass is carried over into the next scene when Rita is late for her tutorial because she has joined in with a discussion with students 'down on the lawn'.

Frank   What's that?

Rita   What?

Frank   On your back.

Rita (*reaching up*)   Oh – it's grass.

Frank   Grass?

Rita   Yeh, I got here early today. I started talking to some students down on the lawn. (p. 64)

In the film version Rita is on her way to the tutorial and is accosted by Tyson and asked to settle an argument about Lawrence's early work. This cuts to a shot of Frank looking out of his study window and witnessing the scene taking place.

In *Breezeblock Park*, Sandra becomes exasperated because Betty, her mother, has decided that it would be best now that Sandra is pregnant for her and her partner Tim to come and live at home with them. This is in direct conflict with Sandra's own feelings because she wants to move in with Tim, which she sees as her chance to escape from the confines of her working-class family.

Sandra   I want a *good* life, Mother. I want something that's got some meaning left init. I want to sit around and talk about films and – and music. I want a house where we don't have the telly on all day, where we don't worry about the furniture. I want books on the shelves. Mother – and – oh – for God's

> sake, I want paintings on the wall and red wine on the table
> and lots of different cheeses. I want – I want – I want . . .
> (*Breezeblock Park*, Act Two)

In this speech, there is a hint of the kind of life that Rita says
she is after too and Sandra is an embryonic form of Willy
Russell's later creation. Rita's interests extend to literature
and, although she knows it is the 'proper thing' to take wine
to a dinner party, one of the reasons she gives in Act One,
Scene Six, for not turning up at Frank's house is that she
knew she had bought the wrong wine.

In *Daughters of Albion,* three girls who work in a biscuit
factory, find themselves at the wrong all-night party. This
gives Willy Russell a context in which these working-class
characters can mix with the middle classes and one of the
girls, Kathleen, is offered the opportunity by one of the
students to escape from her current life.

> She's interesting, Kathleen, I still love her because she's got no
> humour. She's great. She's just one of those women who's spot
> on and cuts through everything. She never laughs, terribly
> intense, serious girl, but she wants to know what's going on – I
> just love her. Very Liverpool type. (Russell in Gill, 1992, p. 60)

Unlike Rita and Linda in *Stags and Hens*, Kathleen is unable
to make the break from her working-class roots and her
friends to explore a new kind of life. Linda is about to get
married to Dave in *Stags and Hens*. The play takes place in
the gents' and ladies' toilets and the corridor in between in a
Liverpool dance hall. The friends of the bride and the
groom have managed to book their respective stag and hen
parties at the same venue. Linda at age twenty-two is
destined for the married life that Rita finds herself in:

> **Linda**   Y' do get frightened y' know. I mean if it was just
> gettin' married to Dave it'd be OK, he's all right Dave is. But
> it's like, honest, it's like I'm gettin' married to a town . . . It's
> not just like I'm marryin' Dave. It's like if I marry him I marry
> everythin'. Like, I could sit down now an' draw you a chart of
> everythin' that'll happen in my life after tomorrow. (*Stags and
> Hens*, Act One)

Linda meets Peter, her ex-boyfriend, who is on the road

with the band that is playing at the stag and hen party. Peter left Liverpool for London and at the time he had asked Linda to join him. Peter says to Linda, 'Stay around here if y' want to Linda. Have y' kids an' keep y' mates an' go dancin' an' go to the pub an' go to the shops an' do all those things you used to tell me you hated doing' (Act Two). This serves as a reminder to her of what getting married and staying in Liverpool will mean and, at the end of the play, she escapes through the gents' toilet window to take Peter up on his offer of a lift in the band's van.

While these earlier plays are works in their own right, it is as though the character of Rita is there as a shadow in the background and Willy Russell was working through several versions of her until the girl he wanted to explore becomes fully formed in *Educating Rita*.

As with most writers, there are aspects of autobiography in Willy Russell's work but the characters in his play are the result of the creative working out of ideas. In his imagination he has distilled events, speech and the characteristics of people from his experience but ultimately he is a dramatist who has used the elements of stagecraft to fashion a workable and effective piece of drama. The decision to make Rita a hairdresser may have been informed by the fact that Willy Russell was himself a hairdresser but she is not based on any particular hairdresser he knows. Similarly, Willy Russell was himself a teacher and has been taught by the Franks of this world, and this experience is used imaginatively to make Frank a credible character. To some extent, the transformation that education makes to Rita's life is something that Willy Russell experienced by returning to education in his twenties. Education and the resultant move from being a manual worker to becoming a teacher and then a writer have provided Willy Russell with the wherewithal and the choice to join the 'cultured' classes.

> There was no conscious attempt to sit and sculpt out an autobiographical play. I mean, I loot my past, as anyone does. The reason Rita's a hairdresser is that I could sketch her outside life with some authority; without having to conduct

research – the greatest excuse for not writing ever. (Russell in
an interview with Rob Kinsman, 2004)

The parallel between Willy Russell's personal experience
and ambition and that of Rita must partly account for the
sincerity of the writing and the believability of Rita as a
character, but it is also his imaginative gift as a writer which
has produced a character who so readily comes to life when
interpreted and portrayed by an actor.

The play was written in Willy Russell's father-in-law's
book-lined study and something like it became the setting
for the play and the stimulus for the idea of making the
action happen in a tutorial situation between a university
lecturer and his student. Although the idea for the play took
some time in coming, Willy Russell recalls how 'one
afternoon, Rita just walked on to the page and stayed. I
didn't ask where she came from, what she was doing, what
the play was about – I just kept writing' (interview with
Philip Key, *Liverpool Daily Post*, 2002).

The fact that Willy Russell 'just kept writing' and did not
conduct any detailed research about the Open University
may account for the lack of verisimilitude in relation to the
way in which teaching on these courses actually occurs (see
note about the Open University on p. 84). Also it is doubtful
whether anyone with the level of education that Rita has
could go straight on to the sort of course that Frank is
teaching.

Frank   You've barely had a basic schooling, you've never
even sat a formal examination let alone passed one. Possessing
a hungry mind is not in itself a guarantee of any kind of
success. (p. 27)

The interesting thing is that, while it is a criticism that can
be levelled at the play, no one actually seems to mind, least
of all the Open University which awarded Willy Russell an
honorary masters degree in 1983. In the film, Rita can be
seen using a copy of the actual Open University study guide
to *Peer Gynt* and watching an Open University programme.
The point is that the Open University provides a pretext for
someone like Rita to return to education and for the tutorial

situation to be used as the theatrical device which enables the story of *Educating Rita* to be told.

Genre

Educating Rita is described as a comedy, although Willy Russell does not necessarily consider himself to be a writer of comedies. When he is 'comin' on with the funnies' (as Rita says, p. 49), these arise naturally out of the circumstances surrounding the dramatic situation and are part of the inherent make-up of the characters. The play is not written primarily for laughs.

> I am not a witty man . . . but what happens is, if I get the characters right, the wit emerges out of the characters. As I say, I'm not a funny man, I love wit, I love witty people and I really admire them but I am not, myself. (Russell in Gill, 1992, p. 66).

Michael Billington wrote after the first performance that 'I honestly found the opening gruesome with its endless parade of easy gags ("Do you know Yeats?" – "You mean the wine lodge").' This comment overlooks the purpose of the gags, which are Rita's way initially of dealing with her nervousness in finding herself in unfamiliar circumstances and in the presence of an academic. When Rita returns from the summer school, her feelings of being inadequate within the hallowed circles of academia have all but disappeared and she has acquired a new confidence. This change is apparent in the way that she explains to Frank how she resisted using the type of gag that Billington finds so gruesome:

> **Rita**   Anyway, this tutor come up to me, he looked at the book in me hand an' he said, 'Ah, are you fond of Ferlinghetti?' It was right on the tip of me tongue to say, 'Only when it's served with Parmesan cheese', but, Frank, I didn't. I held it back an' I heard meself sayin', 'Actually, I'm not too familiar with the American poets.' (p. 55)

Nevertheless, it is a funny moment for the audience and for

Frank by the very fact that she is reporting what she did not do. At the same time, we also admire Rita for recognising the importance of modifying her behaviour to suit the circumstances.

It is true to say that there is plenty of humour in *Educating Rita* and audiences find a lot to laugh at, but there is also a vein of seriousness that runs throughout the play. One of the defining characteristics of a genuine comedy is that there should be a happy ending. While the ending of *Educating Rita* is quite upbeat with the resolution of Rita's threat at the end of Act One, Scene One, to give Frank a haircut, the future for Frank is a form of academic exile in the Antipodes and the outcome for Rita, while potentially positive, is uncertain. The American producers of the film wanted it to have a definite happy ending and tried to insist that Rita should fly off into the sunset with Frank but as Michael Caine, who played Frank in the film, writes,

> Higgins and Liza [characters from Shaw's *Pygmalion*, to which *Educating Rita* is often compared; Caine is referring to the 'happy ending' musical version, *My Fair Lady*] are both attractive people who wind up falling in love with each other, but I didn't see *Educating Rita* in this way at all. I saw it with an under-theme of an ugly professor (he is an alcoholic in the story) who has an unrequited love for an attractive student. (Caine, 1992, p. 397)

Caine's view of the play suggests that it is also a love story, which is what Willy Russell himself has said he set out to write.

> I hope you will not think me lowbrow, unsound or inferior when I tell you that when making *Educating Rita* I tried very hard to write a love story. (Russell/Glaap, 1997, p. 6)

If it is a love story, from Rita's point of view, any feelings of love are purely platonic and the relationship which develops is one of mutual respect between an older, educated man and a woman thirty years his junior who has a real thirst for knowledge. There is undoubtedly an attraction between the two protagonists, but it is on the level of flirtation and innuendo rather than with any intention of

taking it into the realms of a romantic or sexual relationship.
It could be called an almost-love story in that throughout
the play there is a sense of anticipation about whether or not
Rita and Frank might fall in love. Rita makes it quite clear
to Frank that she thinks of him as her teacher when he
suggests that Denny might be thinking that she is having an
affair with him. And Frank points out later in the scene that
his partner, Julia, might not look too favourably upon Rita's
invitation to him to go to the theatre with her. In this
interchange, there is also a clear sense of playfulness in their
relationship which comes through the jokes and shows how
comfortable they are in each other's company.

Frank   [. . .] And how would I explain that to Julia?

Rita   Just tell her y' comin' to the theatre with me.

Frank   'Julia, I shall not be in for dinner tonight as I am
going to the theatre with ravishing Rita.'

Rita   Oh, sod off.

Frank   I'm being quite serious.

Rita   Would she really be jealous?

Frank   If she knew I was at the theatre with an irresistible
thing like you? Rita, it would be deaf-and-dumb breakfasts for
a week.

Rita   Why?

Frank   Why not?

Rita   I dunno – I just thought . . .

Frank   Rita, as ludicrous as it may seem to you, even a
woman who possesses an MA is not above common jealousy.

Rita   Well, what's she got to be jealous of me for? I'm not
gonna rape y' in the middle of *The Seagull*.

Frank   What a terrible pity. You just might have made
theatre exciting for me again. (p. 40)

What is crucial to appreciating Willy Russell's work is the
fact that he sets out to tell a story and a story that has an
immediate appeal to an audience. While it is possible to find

all sorts of symbolic meaning in the play or to explain its purpose as social documentary, it is the primacy and immediacy of the story that make it the type of play that it is.

> The story, the narrative, which is unfashionable in the study of English Literature, is to me all-important. A story, like a song, can transcend barriers of language, class and race.
> Sophisticates are suspicious of stories, believing that stories are only for children or the simple-minded. But a story is a difficult thing to make. It is a primal and magic thing and cannot be made by those who've turned their backs on simplicity.
> (Russell/Glaap, 1997, pp. 5–6)

In this respect, *Educating Rita* is a drama that just happens to be funny. The comedy is a consequence of the narrative. The interactions between Frank and Rita as their story unfolds through their dialogue and actions produce an effect that is intrinsically amusing. It is convenient to describe the play as a comedy for marketing purposes as this gives it a wider audience appeal but, rather like the so-called comedies of Alan Ayckbourn, there is a subtle vein of seriousness that permeates its fabric.

To date, Willy Russell's main body of work as a playwright falls into the two broad categories of either naturalistic drama or musical theatre. In *Educating Rita*, though it falls into the first category, there is no attempt to create a literal or accurate picture of reality: Willy Russell is presenting a fictionalised version of an Open University tutorial. He is giving the audience his take on how he imagines the story to develop between a more or less permanently inebriated fifty-something university professor and a twenty-six-year-old Scouse hairdresser. The 'magic' of *Educating Rita* is the way in which Russell tells his story and how it comes to life on stage. Although Rita and Frank are fictional characters, they have to be believable for an audience to empathise with their particular human condition and relationship. For this to happen, actors approaching the roles are required to find a reality to their playing that will ensure an artistic truth. The play calls for a naturalistic style of acting and within each scene the unities of time, space and action are observed.

Throughout the play, there is no obvious attempt to break the 'fourth wall' and in this respect it is entirely naturalistic. The audience might as well be other books on the shelves as, in a stylistic sense, there is no conscious acknowledgement of its presence by the characters. From an actor's point of view however, the audience's reaction to the play has a major impact on the timing and pace of the dialogue and it is this dimension that it is almost impossible to capture just from a reading of the script.

Structure

The earlier plays, *Breezeblock Park* (1975) and *One for the Road* (1976/1987), served as a kind of rehearsal for *Educating Rita* and provided the opportunity for Willy Russell to develop and refine both his playwriting skills and his knowledge of stagecraft by writing within the confines of a naturalistic structure. Act One of *Breezeblock Park* takes place on Christmas Eve in the sitting room and kitchen of one house and Act Two takes place the next day in another, different but very similar, house.

> I do like to be clever with the stage. I mean, there was something in *Breezeblock Park* which never ever worked really and yet I loved the idea of it – the idea that the house in Act One is merely the reverse of the house in Act Two, so that you show immediately that Betty and Reeny have cancelled themselves out, they have identical houses. But in fact what happens is the curtain goes up for the second act and I'm sure that the audience think that the producers haven't got much money so what they've just done is turned the set around.
> (Russell in Gill, 1992, p. 61)

Within each act, the action plays in more or less 'real' time and is continuous. With nine characters the combinations of interactions are more varied and the narrative is conveyed by a wider range of voices than in *Educating Rita*. The greatest challenge in this play is to invent convincing ways of getting characters on and off stage.

One for the Road has just the one setting which is Dennis
and Pauline's lounge. Dennis and Pauline are having their
neighbours, Roger and Jane, over for dinner with Dennis's
parents. A conceit which runs through the play is that all of
the bungalows on the newly built estate, with its streets
named after classical composers, look the same and the
parents, who cannot find the place, are constantly phoning
up asking for directions. The play takes place over one
evening and the only shift in time is between the two acts
when, having burnt the casserole they were having for
dinner, they have sent out for and eaten a Chinese
takeaway. The telephone and conversations with unheard
and unseen neighbours out of the window are used to
introduce new information into the story and to move the
plot along.

Unlike these two earlier plays, the story of *Educating Rita*
takes place over a much more extended period of time.

> I was always worried about the structure of *Educating Rita*. It
> has form, it has the unity of time and space – but in a way that
> was not immediately obvious to me when I wrote it. And when
> I saw it I thought, oh yes, it goes over an arc of a year, or
> whatever, or an arc of three years, however you want to see it.
> It just had to be written in consecutive scenes. (Russell/Glaap,
> 1997, p. 106)

Each scene represents a snapshot of 'real time' within the
year or so that it takes Rita to pass her first exams. The two
clear anchor points in the play are the summer school which
takes place between Acts One and Two and the fact that in
the last scene Rita is 'wrapped in a large winter coat' and
has come to wish Frank a Merry Christmas. For the West
End transfer, the notion of the action of the play starting
in January and ending in December within a year was
added but this need not necessarily be the case. The play
obviously begins at the beginning of a university term and it
is possible to start an Open University module in late
September/early October or January. The first four scenes
of Act One all take place in the evening and provide a
developmental glimpse into the tutorial process over an

unspecified period of time. Act One, Scene Five, takes place at lunchtime when Rita makes an impromptu visit to see Frank to share her enthusiasm with him over the production of *Macbeth* she has been to see. The first part of Rita's course involves her writing a critical appreciation of *Rubyfruit Jungle* and studying *Howards End*, *Peer Gynt* and *The Seagull* which, if considered literally, is a fairly tall order for one term's work when she has had no previous literary education.

Act One ends with Rita's renewed determination to succeed at her studies and there is a clear indication that there are more tutorials to follow with Frank before she embarks on the summer school.

> **Rita** [. . .] You've just gorra keep tellin' me an' then I'll start to take it in; y'see, with me you've got to be dead firm. You won't hurt me feelings, y'know. If I do somethin' that's crap, I don't want pity, you just tell me, 'That's crap'. Here, it's crap. Right. So we dump that in the bin, an' we start again. (p. 53)

There is an enormous step-change between the two acts of the play. The interval therefore has a real significance in providing an imagined space for Rita to progress with her learning and gain the experience that enables her to discuss Blake's poetry and compare *Sons and Lovers* and *Lady Chatterley's Lover* with informed confidence. Whatever the time lapse between the acts, the second half of the play begins in the autumn and arcs towards Rita's exams in late November, culminating with her gaining the results in December and saying her farewell to Frank before he leaves for Australia. As a whole, the structure of the play reflects the chronological order of sequential teaching sessions and Willy Russell has selected fourteen key scenes from the developing relationship between Frank and Rita to present to the audience. The play works in performance just as much by what Willy Russell has chosen to leave to the audience's imagination between the scenes as by what he has decided to present on stage. This is where the stage and film versions of the story differ significantly.

The technical exercise Willy Russell sets himself in *Educating Rita* is far more ambitious than in anything that he had written up to this point because of the restrictions of the duologue form. In fact in the first draft of the play sent to Peggy Ramsay, his agent, he had virtually written it as monologue for Rita.

> I'd written *Rita* and I didn't want anybody else's voice to get in the way. I had to write her story, her voice. So in that original draft Frank was an absolute vapid, colourless, almost off-stage cipher, a totally colourless man. Just occasionally he'd throw in a question or something in order to propel Rita's journey along further. He was an absolute foil. Having completed this first draft in which I'd completely realised Rita, I sent it to Peggy [. . .] She had read it and she thought Rita was wonderful and Frank totally useless. I was crushed, because it had taken me so long to write this play, not long in terms of time but it had taken so much out of me. The thought of having to go back to it depressed me beyond belief. It took me about eighteen or twenty hours before starting to think, 'What I've got to do is I've got to write this play again, I've got to conceive Frank.' [. . .] I put the paper into the typewriter and instinctively I knew that if I was going to get Frank right, the play had to start with him. I was suddenly thrilled because I had a character here, not just a cipher. (Russell/Glaap, 1997, pp. 109–10)

It is hard to imagine the play without Frank as the counterpoint to Rita's character and without the repartee between the two of them. Six years later, Willy Russell went on to use the monologue form to outstanding effect in *Shirley Valentine*.

One of the constraints of a single-set, two-character, naturalistic drama like *Educating Rita* is the fact that reported speech becomes the main means of conveying events and information from the off-stage world. It is testimony to Willy Russell's skill as a dramatist that this is achieved in a way which is both dramatically convincing and occurs naturally in the dialogue rather than sounding contrived. There are only three ways the audience receives information from beyond the world of the tutorial room and these are via Frank, Rita and the telephone. Rita is the main 'bringer of news' as she is nearly always the one to enter the room. In nine out of the play's fourteen scenes Rita enters the room

with Frank already *in situ*, two scenes begin with both of
them in the room, two scenes have Rita in the room with
Frank entering afterwards and the remaining scene is the
short phone conversation Frank has when he is trying to
contact Rita about her examination.

The opening scene runs for some twenty minutes in
performance and constitutes about one third of the first half
of the play. It functions as the exposition of both plot and
character and packs in a considerable amount of
information so that the rest of the scenes can become
developmental episodes that spring from this initial idea.

When the lights come up for the first time, the audience is
transported to a book-lined room and Frank immediately
hints at the fact that he is an English Literature lecturer by
calling out the names of famous authors. Hidden behind
these symbols of academia, however, is the evidence of the
fact that he has a drinking habit. The telephone only
features twice as a dramatic device and its use in this first
scene provides the audience with the information that Frank
has a partner named Julia and that he is working late
because he has 'got this Open University woman coming'. It
also signals the fact that his relationship with Julia is
somewhat antagonistic and that life on the domestic front is
far from being a state of bliss.

Rita's characteristics of loquaciousness and having few
social graces provide Willy Russell with an intrinsically
convincing way of introducing plot information. The set-up
of a student attending her first tutorial allows Frank to ask
her name: 'Now, you are?' but Rita circumvents the
expected response by saying, 'What am I?' This delays the
formal introductions while Frank finds his admission papers
and Rita finds a distraction in the nude painting on the
study wall. Frank hardly gets a word in during this initial
encounter and it is deliberately written for Rita to make an
impression on Frank and the audience. The technique of
Rita asking and answering most of her own questions as a
character trait provides Willy Russell with a realistic
convention that enables him to communicate information
about her background through her own words. Rita admits

to Frank that she has been testing him to see how he would
react to her:

Rita   Know if I'd got some other tutor I wouldn't have
stayed.

Frank   What do you mean, another tutor?

Rita   Y'know, someone who objected to swearin'.

Frank   How did you know that I wouldn't object?

Rita   I didn't. I was just testin' y'. (p. 9)

It is only once Rita and Frank's relationship has been
established and some of the character detail has been
sketched in that we find out who these people are. But even
the potentially straightforward exchange of names becomes
an extended episode of word play and allusion to other
literary works. Frank's official paperwork has his new
student's name down as 'Mrs S. White', but Rita explains to
him that she has changed her name in homage to the author
of her favourite book, *Rubyfruit Jungle* by Rita Mae Brown.
When Frank tells Rita his name, she asks if he was named
after someone too and this leads to the discussion about
Eliot Ness and T.S. Eliot. Towards the end of the scene the
tension is built up to the point where Rita leaves after Frank
has told her he is an appalling teacher. Without Rita's
decision and determination to return there would of course
be no play, but Willy Russell uses this as a moment to show
how, despite their cultural, class, social and educational
differences, they are a well-matched pair. It is the dramatic
potential created in this clash of personalities that Willy
Russell explores, exploits and resolves in the subsequent
scenes of the play.

Rita

Rita's entrance into Frank's study is frustrated by the faulty
door handle. But her persistent knocking and almost forced
entry are emblematic of what motivates the character.
When Frank's study door opens to reveal Rita framed in the

doorway both he and audience are presented with something of a visual and aural incongruity. The fact that the play opens with Frank means that the audience has had time to take in the book-lined study with its academic paraphernalia and his reading out the names of some of the great and the good of English literature establishes a certain expectation of restrained and well-mannered intellectual debate. Of course students are apt to wear unconventional and bizarre clothing but Rita's outfit somehow looks out of place and as soon as she opens her mouth to speak, her accent reveals that she is probably 'uneducated'. It is not only the way Rita looks and how she sounds that sets her apart from Frank's world but what she says and the way she says it. Both her accent and her dialect define her, or rather they did for an audience in 1980s London. It is hard to imagine the impact on the original audience of having a female character speaking in a Liverpudlian accent taking centre stage in the mainly middle-class land of West End theatre. To use Rita's expression, they were probably gobsmacked. But just as Rita wins Frank over, the character wins over the audience too.

Once in the room, she makes an immediate impression on both the audience and Frank. All of the usual social niceties are dispensed with as she swears and curses her way into Frank's world of academia: 'that stupid bleeding handle', 'poor bastard on the other side of the door'. The juxtaposing of a working-class character speaking in a regional accent with the hallowed inner sanctum of a university tutorial room states the two central themes of the play: education and the class divide. More exactly, the play sets out to demonstrate through Rita's voice and actions how gaining an education can be a transforming experience for an individual by providing an escape route from the perceived limitations of her working-class roots to the wider opportunities afforded to and by the middle classes. While it might be possible to read some sort of sociological thesis into the play, Willy Russell's primary intention is to tell the story of one individual's attempt to better herself. It is a personal journey for Rita but one with which many individuals who have seen the play and the film will have found a great degree of empathy.

Rita's entrance creates an immediate fascination and interest for an audience. She is like a firework going off, with her swearing, her forthright questions and her apparent disregard for any social graces. She launches straight into things that are on her mind and gives her opinion whether she is asked for it or not. Her way of dealing with Frank is to talk at him and over him. Far from exhibiting any deference for his academic position and status, Rita fills the silences with conversation about anything that comes to mind. In order to relax in Frank's company, Rita is very soon smoking a cigarette and joining him in a drink as though their meeting were a social gathering rather than their first tutorial in English literature.

Rita's talkativeness at the start of the play ('I talk too much don't I? Just tell me to shut up if I go on too much') is partly born of her nervousness at being in a new situation with her potential teacher and partly an indicator of her overwhelming enthusiasm for learning about things beyond her present experience. Rita's affinity with language is apparent in the way that she picks up on the meaning and sounds of words and they are a source of much of the comedy in the play. She turns the title of *Howards End* into a *double-entendre* and she is quick to make a pun of the novelist's name when she asks 'Forced her to do what'? Willy Russell exploits the similarity between the name of the Irish poet and playwright W.B. Yeats and the chain of wine bars (Yates') to provide a witty illustration of the difference between Rita's experiences of the vernacular and Frank's more rarefied acquaintance with a literary and more cultured figure. There is surprise, as much for the audience as for Frank, at the speed with which she is quick to learn a concept like assonance. It is doubly witty because she explains it back to him by giving him an example from the vernacular: wink/wank.

The main facts about Rita are that her real name is Susan White, aged twenty-six and married to Denny. They have been trying to have a baby for over two years. Denny wants

a child but Rita does not and she is in fact still on the pill.
Rita works as a ladies' hairdresser but hates the job and is
not particular good at it. The name she has given herself is
based on her favourite novelist, Rita Mae Brown. The
choice of name is significant because Rita obviously sees a
parallel between the life and background of Molly in
Rubyfruit Jungle and her own.

> Molly is my daughter, and if it's the last thing I do, I'm going
> to see that girl gets a chance in this world neither one of us
> had. You want her to spend her life like us, sitting back here in
> the sticks, can't even make enough money for a new dress or
> dinner in a restaurant? You want her to live a life like you –
> dishes, cooking, and never going out except maybe to a movie
> once a month if we can afford it? The child's got brightness in
> her, so let her be! She'll go to big cities and be somebody. I
> can see it in her. She's got dreams and ambition and she's
> smart as a whip. Nobody can pull one over on that kid. Be
> proud of her. (*Rubyfruit Jungle*, pp. 40–1)

'She's got dreams and ambition and she's smart as a whip'
could just as well describe Rita. When she first walks into
Frank's life she does not feel comfortable or at ease being
called Susan White. It is as if she has to leave Susan at the
hairdresser's and at home with Denny and take on another
persona to convince herself that she is good enough for a
university education. By the second act, when she has given
up hairdressing, left Denny, is living in a flat with Trish and
working at a bistro, Rita has found the independence and
confidence to be known as Susan. Her education and
cultural experiences have enabled her to evolve into the
Susan she wants to be and not the life that her parents and
husband had mapped out for her. The sad thing is that she
allows Frank to continue calling her Rita and in her anger
she uses it against him to assert her eventual emancipation
from him: 'Nobody calls me Rita but you. I dropped that
pretentious crap as soon as I saw it for what it was' (p. 77).

Rita looks to education to change her life. In the words of
Dorothy Fields, Rita feels that 'there's gotta be something
better than this'. She wants to be able to appreciate what
she calls 'culture', which she associates with 'the educated'

as opposed to 'the masses'. She even makes a distinction between the way in which people of her class and background use swear words out of ignorance and the more knowing way the upper classes supposedly use them: 'I say, the grouse is particularly fucking lovely today although I'm afraid the spuds are a bit bollocks, don't you think?' George Bernard Shaw would have us believe that it is not the English language itself that defines class but accents and regional dialects. If this were the case and Rita was cast as Eliza Doolittle and Frank as Professor Higgins, one of his first tasks would be to eradicate her Liverpudlian accent and to correct her use of the Scouse dialect, neither of which he attempts to do. In fact when Rita arrives in Act Two, Scene Two, 'speaking properly', as she calls it, Frank insists that she speak in her normal voice. While an Oxbridge or public school accent may still be associated with the highly educated and the sophisticated, it is not necessarily the hallmark of the intelligentsia or the cultured any longer.

It is possible to track Rita's journey from literary ignorance to enlightenment through the eight milestone speeches she has in the play. In the first she explains how she has arrived at her decision to seek out an education:

Oh it's not sudden. I've been realisin' for ages that I was . . . slightly out of step. I'm twenty-six. I should have had a baby by now; everyone expects it – I'm sure my husband thinks I'm infertile. He's always goin' on about havin' babies. We've been tryin' for two years now; but I'm still on the pill! See, I don't want a baby yet. I wanna find myself first, discover myself. Do you understand that? (**Frank** *nods.*) Yeh. They wouldn't round our way. I've tried to explain it to my husband but between you an' me I think he's just thick! No, not *thick*; blind, that's what he is. He can't see, because he doesn't *want* to see. If I try an' do anything different he get's a gob on him; even if I'm just reading or watchin' somethin' different on the telly he gets really narked. I just used to tell him to piss off but then I realised it was no good just doin' that an' what I should do is try an' explain to him. An' I tried; I tried explainin' to him how I wanted a better way of livin' my life. For once he listened. An' I even believed he understood because he said he felt the same as me – but all he meant was he was fed up livin'

on our estate so we should start saving and try and move out
to somewhere like Formby. Formby! Jesus, even if it was a new
house I wanted I wouldn't move out to Formby. I hate that
hole. Don't you? (p. 14)

Having recognised her difference and the need to discover
herself, the next stage in Rita's development and process of
self-realisation is to find a way of escaping from the world
she knows to one that promises something different. In it
there is also a sad indictment of the kind of education that is
experienced by young people in secondary schools and how
they can easily be turned off by it. It is also a reminder that
in the kind of youth culture that Willy Russell is writing
about the idea of taking school and learning seriously goes
against the overriding need for credibility, for belonging to
'y' gang of mates'.

See, if I'd started takin' school seriously then I would have had
to become different from my mates . . . So y' never admit that
school could be anythin' other than useless an' irrelevant. An'
what you've really got to be into are things like music an'
clothes and gettin' pissed an' coppin' off an' all that kind of
stuff. Not that I didn't go along with it because I did. But at
the same time, there was always somethin' tappin' away in my
head, tryin' to tell me I might have got it all wrong. But I'd
just put the music back on or buy another dress an' stop
worryin'. 'Cos there's always something that can make y'
forget. An' so y' keep on goin', tellin' y'self that life is great –
there's always another club to go to, a new feller to be chasin',
a laugh an' a joke with the girls. Till one day, you just stop an'
own up to yourself. Y' say, 'Is this it? Is this the absolute
maximum that I can expect from this livin' lark?' An' that's
the really big moment that is. Because that is when you've got
to decide whether it's gonna be another change of dress or a
change in yourself. And it's really tempting to go out an get
that other dress. Because that way it's easy; y' know that you
won't be upsettin' anyone or hurtin' anyone – apart from
y'self! An' sometimes it's easier to do that, to take the pain
y'self instead of hurtin' those around y'; those who don't want
you to change. (p. 19)

In her twenties, Rita seems to have reached an early mid-life
crisis. Asking herself the big philosophical questions, 'what is

life all about?' and 'why are we here?' is bound to play on
the mind of one so young. Rita's next important speech is
the only overtly political pronouncement in the play and the
closest that Willy Russell gets to pushing home any social
message. The revised ending to the speech reflects the
playwright's own feelings about the direction in which
society appears to be travelling. According to Glen Walford
who directed the 2002 Liverpool revival, 'He [Willy Russell]
included this new speech about the Got-to-Have culture
which has changed since the eighties. Technology has gone
on at such a pace that people have got to have the things
like trainers and wide screen televisions, something I know
Willy hates and which horrifies him. So he wrote that into it
so it packs even more of a punch now' (quoted in Philip
Key, 'Coming Back to Rita is All the Sweeter', *Liverpool Daily
Post*, 8 November 2002). Rita equates materialism with a
kind of disease that masks the real issues in society. There is
a certain nostalgia about the speech, looking back at a pre-
war generation that did not have much in the way of wealth
and possessions, at a time when there was a real sense of
community and when people looked out for one another.
Rita can see around her that people own their houses and
have the latest gadgets and yet they are prepared to ignore
the vandalism and social unrest that surrounds them. It is
important to remember that when the play was written the
Toxteth race riots of 1979 were fresh in people's memories
and there was a considerable amount of civil unrest in the
city. Liverpool has come a long way in thirty years from
being a city in crisis with 'no-go' areas to the European
Capital of Culture in 2008.

> There is no contentment. Because there's no meanin' left.
> (*Beat.*) Sometimes, when y' hear the old ones tellin' stories
> about the past, y' know about the war or when they were all
> strugglin', fightin' for food and clothes and houses, their eyes
> light up while they're tellin' y' because there *was* some meanin'
> then. But what's . . . what's stupid is that *now* . . . now that
> most of them have got some kind of a house an' there is food
> an' money around, they're better off but, honest, they know
> they've got nothin' as well – because the meanin's all gone; so

there's nothin' to believe in. It's like there's this sort of disease but no one mentions it; everyone behaves as though it's normal, y' know inevitable, that there's vandalism an' violence an' houses burnt out and wrecked by the people they were built for. But this disease, it just keeps on bein' hidden; because everyone's caught up in the 'Got-to-Have' game, all runnin' round like headless chickens chasin' the latest got-to-have tellies an' got-to-have cars, got-to-have haircuts an' got-to-have phones an' all the other got-to-have garbage that leaves y' wonderin' why you've still got nothin' – even when you've got it. (*Beat.*) I suppose it's just like me isn't it, y' know when I was buyin' dresses – keepin' the disease covered up all the time. (p. 32)

There is sadness and pain in the way that Rita's personal life crumbles around her. She has to come to terms with the fact that she no longer loves Denny because they cannot give each other the kind of things in life that each wants. As much as she tries to hold her marriage together, the fact that she wants bigger and wider choices out of life than her husband means that they have become incompatible and their eventual break-up is an inevitable consequence of her seeking an education for herself. The speech shows that there is fondness between Rita and Denny but however much he tries to rekindle their relationship she knows that she can never go back. There is a genuine kindness in the way that she talks about Denny and a humanity about the way she realises that she has to let him go and that he is completely blameless.

I see him lookin' at me sometimes, an' I know what he's thinkin'; he's wonderin' where the girl he married has gone to. He even brings me presents sometimes, hopin' that the presents'll make her come back. But she can't, because she's gone, an' I've taken her place [. . .]

[. . .] But it's *not* takin' the place of life, it's *providin'* me with life. He wants to take life away from me; he wants me to stop rockin' the coffin, that's all. Comin' here, doin' this, it's given me more life than I've had in years, an' he should be able to see that. Well, if he doesn't see that, if he doesn't want me when I'm alive, then I'm certainly not just gonna lie down an' die for him. I told him I'd only have a baby when I had a

choice. But he doesn't understand. He thinks we've got choice
because we can go into a pub that sells eight different kinds of
lager. He thinks we've got choice already: choice between
Everton an' Liverpool, choosin' which washin' powder,
choosin' between one shitty school an' the next, between jobs
for jokers or stayin' on the dole. He thinks we've *got* choice
already because there's thirty-eight satellite channels on to
watch. (p. 37)

There is a pivotal point in the play when Rita realises that
she has become a complete outsider. She no longer belongs
to the world in which she has grown up but neither does she
yet belong to the world of dinner parties and educated
conversation. There is a wonderful pathos in the way that
Rita recognises in her mother's unhappiness, that the life of
singing songs in the local boozer is no longer the life for her
and that she can drop the pretence of having ever enjoyed
it.

Rita   I'm all right with you, here in this room; but when I
saw those people you were with I couldn't come in. I would
have seized up. Because I'm a freak. I can't talk to the people I
live with any more. An' I can't talk to the likes of them on
Saturday, or them out there, because I can't learn the
language. I'm an alien. I went back to the pub where Denny
was, an' me mother, an' our Sandra, an' her mates. I'd
decided I wasn't comin' here again. I went into the pub an'
they were singin', all of them singin' some song they'd learnt
from the juke-box. An' I stood in that pub an' thought, just
what in the name of Christ am I trying to do? Why don't I just
pack it in, stay with them, an' join in with the singin'?

Frank   And why don't you?

Rita   You think I can, don't you? Just because you pass a
pub doorway an' hear the singin' you think we're all OK, that
we're all survivin', with the spirit intact. Well I *did* join in with
the singin', I didn't ask any questions, I just went along with it.
But when I looked round my mother had stopped singin', an'
she was cryin'. Everyone just said she was pissed an' we should
get her home. So we did, an' on the way I asked her why. I
said, 'Why are y' cryin', Mother?' She said, 'Because – because
we could sing better songs than those.' Ten minutes later,
Denny had her laughing and singing again, pretending she

hadn't said it. But she had. And that's why I came back. And that's why I'm staying. (p. 49)

This is the moment of her firm resolve, when there is no turning back. From this point forward her new life begins and the Rita who used to sum up a painting by saying 'Look at those tits' is now saying 'Tryin' to compare *Chatterley* with *Sons and Lovers* is like tryin' to compare sparkling wine with champagne'. Her description of what she was like at the summer school encapsulates the change in her behaviour and illustrates her new-found confidence, knowledge and enthusiasm for literature.

Y' know at first I was dead scared. I didn't know anyone. I was gonna come home. But the first afternoon I was standin' in the library, y' know lookin' at the books, pretendin' I was dead clever. Anyway, this tutor come up to me, he looked at the book in me hand an' he said, 'Ah, are you fond of Ferlinghetti?' It was right on the tip of me tongue to say, 'Only when it's served with Parmesan cheese', but, Frank, I didn't. I held it back an' I heard meself sayin', 'Actually. I'm not too familiar with the American poets.' Frank, you woulda been dead proud of me. He started talkin' to me about the Beat poets – we sat around for ages – an' he wasn't even one of my official tutors, y' know. We had to go to this big hall for a lecture, there must have been two thousand of us in there. After he'd finished his lecture this professor asked if anyone had a question, an', Frank, I stood up! (*She stands.*) Honest to God, I stood up, an' everyone's lookin' at me. I don't know what possessed me, I was gonna sit down again, but two thousand people had seen me stand up, so I did it, I asked him the question. (p. 55)

By the middle of the second act, Rita is asking Frank to give her some space and indicating that she is different to the person who first walked into his life. She is able to do what every teacher both admires and fears: to think for herself.

I – I care for you, Frank . . . But you've got to – to leave me alone a bit. I'm not an idiot now, Frank – I don't need you to hold me hand as much . . . I can – I can do things on me own more now . . . And I am careful. I know what I'm doin'. Just don't – don't keep treatin' me as though I'm the same as when

I first walked in here. I understand now, Frank; I know the difference between – between – Thomas Hardy and Rita Mae Brown. An' you're still treating me as though I'm hung up on *Rubyfruit Jungle*. (*She goes to the swivel chair and sits.*) Just . . . You understand, don't you, Frank? (p. 70)

In Rita's rightful resentment of what Frank has become, she tells him a few home truths. The respect she had for Frank as both a person and as a tutor temporarily evaporates and she speaks to him as her equal. Education has served to give Rita the one thing that Frank lacks, which is happiness.

I'll tell you what you can't bear, Mr Self-Pitying Piss-Artist; what you can't bear is that I am educated now. What's up, Frank, don't y' like me now that the little girl's grown up, now that y' can no longer bounce me on Daddy's knee an' watch me stare back in wide-eyed wonder at everything he has to say? I'm educated, I've got what you have an' y' don't like it because you'd rather see me as the peasant I once was; you're like the rest of them – you like to keep your natives thick, because that way they still look charming and delightful. I don't need you. (*She gets up and picking up her bag moves away from the desk in the direction of the door.*) I know what clothes to wear, what wine to buy, what plays to see, what papers and books to read. I can do without you. (p. 76)

One of the underlying elements in the play is the *frisson* of sexual attraction between Rita and Frank, but it is all one-sided as Rita either ignores Frank's flirtations or makes a joke out of them. Frank describes Rita as 'an irresistible thing' and thinks it a 'terrible pity' that she is not prepared to rape him in the middle of a production of *The Seagull*. He genuinely believes that she is 'funny, delightful and charming' even if Rita does not believe this about herself. Michael Caine describes how in his interpretation of Frank he set out to portray him in such a way that Rita would not be attracted to him.

I grew a beard and gained thirty pounds so that there was no chance that Rita could possibly fancy me. Changing myself physically in this way was a great help, as for the first time in my life I was playing a character with whom I had nothing in common, a man for whose ideas, outlook on life and in particular

his relationships with women, I had absolutely no sympathy.
Any woman who did not requite my love the moment it was
declared, was very soon forgotten. (Caine, 1992, p. 398)

Rita obviously charms most of the men she meets in her
new social circle, judging by Frank's jealous reaction to her
relationships with 'Mr Tyson' and the lecturer she meets at
the summer school. There is a marvellous moment of sexual
tension at the end of the play, when Rita says, 'I never
thought there was anythin' I could give you', and
commands him to sit on a chair. In Frank's mind, and
possibly the audience's, there is the remotest chance that
Rita might be intending to requite his love but instead she
calls on the skills learnt from her former life and proposes to
give him a haircut.

Rita admits she is hungry for education and to change
her life but she may not be entirely prepared for the pain
and the upset. In breaking up with her husband and
choosing a different life for herself, she finds herself bereft of
the culture into which she was born and not quite accepted
into the one to which she aspires. She describes herself as 'a
freak' and 'an alien'; this is how she is feeling as she moves
from the world that is familiar towards one which is
different and new. In 1965, Dennis Potter wrote a television
play called *Stand Up, Nigel Barton* on a similar theme to
Educating Rita. The play is about a working-class lad from a
Nottinghamshire coal-mining village who makes it as a
student to Oxford and eventually in politics. Nigel Barton
experiences much the same feelings of not belonging to his
family or to the upper-class world of Oxford
undergraduates. Both Rita and Nigel inevitably feel conflict
in betraying their cultural and family roots by striving to
join the educated classes that at one and the same time they
despise. Potter's character sums up this dilemma thus:

Nigel No one who has been brought up in a working-class
culture can ever altogether escape, or wish to escape, the
almost suffocating warmth and friendliness of that culture. But
– as soon as you cross the frontiers between one class and
another you feel – I feel – as though you are negotiating a

minefield. Even one's own parents feel that you are judging them, scorning them even. And believe me, I know what I'm talking about. (Scene Thirteen)

For Rita, the end of the play is a new beginning. Frank may have scornfully asked her, 'Found a culture have you, Rita? Found a better song to sing have you?', but her optimism suggests that she may have found the best of both worlds. Her choices at the end of the play are relatively modest: 'I might go to France. I might go to me mother's. I might even have a baby.' It is not the nature of the choices that matter to her at this stage in her life but the simple fact that she is able to make a choice and that the 'educated Rita' will make informed ones.

Frank

The play is as much about educating Frank as it is about educating Rita. There is a tragic flaw in his character, of low self-esteem and self-destructiveness, revealed by his drinking problem and his inability to recognise his own strengths as a teacher. Mark Kingston was the first actor to play the role and he did so without the benefit of the additional back story that the film script provides for any actor approaching the role today. Christopher Hudson in his *Evening Standard* review described Mark Kingston as 'a weary, grey-haired shambling figure in brown corduroy' and as 'a sounding-board for her [Rita's] fears and enthusiasm' (1980). It is quite easy to see how the role can appear as far less interesting than that of Rita because she has most of the best lines and says at least twice as much as Frank. It is a challenging role for an actor because the given circumstances of the character in the play are quite sketchy and it is difficult to avoid a rather stereotypical portrayal as an embittered and disillusioned academic dipsomaniac.

The bare facts about Frank are that he is aged between fifty and fifty-four and a lecturer of English Literature at a northern English university. He is a whisky drinker and lives with a younger woman called Julia who used to be one of his students and is now a colleague at the university. Frank usually likes to spend his evenings in the pub but in order to provide himself with some extra cash he is waiting to tutor his first Open University student. The initial impression of Frank's character is that he is somewhat rude and brusque from the way he speaks to Julia on the telephone. He has already formed a negative attitude towards the additional work he has taken on because he thinks that it is going to be about some 'silly woman's attempts to get into the mind of Henry James or Thomas Hardy'.

When Rita arrives, Frank is slow to catch on to her sense of humour. It is apparent from the little he says to her and his repeated use of 'erm' that he has never met anyone quite like her before and that he does not know quite what to say. In his role as university tutor, Frank should be interviewing Rita but it is as though she is auditioning him to ensure that he is suitable. Whether he means to or not, he allows Rita to smoke, even though he has given up himself, offers her a glass of whisky which she takes, and admits that he does not mind her swearing. By any standards, these are not the conventional rules normally agreed between a teacher and a pupil and they serve to set the unusual parameters in which the relationship between Frank and Rita develops. The possibility that their relationship might become a sexual one is a source of dramatic tension throughout the play. It is apparent from the type of dress that Frank gives Rita as a gift at the end of the play that he had hopes that their relationship might extend beyond the tutorial room into the bedroom.

Rita's assessment of Frank at the beginning of their relationship is that he is a 'crazy mad piss artist who wants to throw his students through the window' but in her frustration with him near the end of the play this description has changed to 'Mr Self-Pitying Piss-Artist'. While this remark may be said in a moment of anger, the succinctness of it provides an honest summation of the kind of person Frank has become. One of the central themes of the play, that of change and transformation, applies equally to Frank as to Rita: it takes someone like Rita to enable him to recognise his excellence as a teacher rather than thinking of himself as a failed poet. Frank's ability as a teacher is first demonstrated by the subtle distinction he makes about language when answering Rita's question about swearing: 'I've never subscribed to the idea that there's such a thing as bad language – only bad *use* of language.' Once Rita has tested Frank out and decided that he is the tutor for her, she very quickly demands from him an explanation of 'assonance'. Frank's ability as a teacher is then demonstrated by the clear way in which he can explain the quite complex concept of assonance and straight away reach for a copy of Yeats's poetry to give an example. He is even more delighted when Rita confirms her understanding of his explanation by summing it up as 'so "assonance" means gettin' the rhyme wrong'.

It doesn't take long for Frank to become entirely enchanted by Rita, partly because he has never met anyone like her before. Although any overt sexual attraction is kept in the background for much of the play, there must be something about Rita's physical appearance as well as her banter that leads Frank to surprise himself by paying her a compliment. In his drunken haze, he finds himself staring at her. Frank's fascination with Rita is summed up when he says 'I think you're really rather marvellous', and having stated that he expects *her* to be committed and serious about her studies, the same could be said of his own attitude towards teaching her. Rita is far from the 'silly woman' he was expecting to teach and from her interest in popular fiction, he has worked out that she has probably never even heard of Thomas Hardy or Henry James. This makes him question whether or not he can take on the job of tutoring her because he will actually have to teach her something. The stage direction says that he '*drinks with a kind of grimness*' and this indicates the kind of schizophrenic effect of his drinking. One moment, Frank's mood can be charming and entertaining and the next it can be sardonic and patronising. The way he turns on Rita at the end of the first scene and says he does not want to teach her is symptomatic of his self-disgust.

Frank realises from the outset of the play that taking on a student like Rita is a huge responsibility and it scares him to death. Beneath the grizzled exterior there is still a moral code. His assumption that he could take on a student as an 'extracurricular activity' purely for monetary gain is questioned right from the outset. Having Rita enter the closeted environment of his book-lined room and opening his eyes after ten years to the fact that the print on his study wall is erotic soon makes him realise that Rita is going to require more of him than his usual *laissez-faire* attitude to teaching. In short, he is going to have to work for a change and earn his salary. Rita may be gobsmacked by the sight of the whisky bottles hidden behind Frank's books but Frank is equally gobsmacked by her forwardness. He has simply never experienced a student who is prepared to look at a painting and say 'Look at those tits'. His reaction to this is to cover his surprise and embarrassment by shuffling the papers on his desk but Rita has unknowingly wrong-footed him and possibly altered the downward trajectory of his life.

At the beginning of the second scene, Frank is sober or at least he is trying to resist the temptation to take a drink. The way in which he keeps looking out of the window and at his watch suggests that he is both excited and anxious about Rita's impending second visit. He might also be partly hoping that he has put her off altogether and that she has heeded his instruction not to come back the following week. Rita's arrival prevents him from taking an early-evening tipple and he spends the whole of his second tutorial with her without going anywhere near the whisky bottle. Unfortunately his longing to have a drink is there in the background because when his patience finally gives out he says, 'Then go back to what you *do* like and stop wasting my time. You go off and buy yourself a new dress and I'll go to the pub!'

Frank's drinking habit is something that has to be finely judged in interpreting the character. Willy Russell's intention was to write a man who drinks heavily but so far it is a habit and not an addiction. The fact that Frank drinks also means that not everything he says can be taken literally.

For Frank, the drink helps to take the edge off his disillusionment and his failed ambition.

> You see Rita, the great thing about the booze is that one is never bored when drinking. Or boring for that matter; the booze has this marvellous capacity for making one believe that underneath all the talk one is actually *saying* something. (p. 38)

In his academic life, Frank has met some degree of success but his personal life is a disaster. In Frank's own words, 'There's a lot less to me than meets the eye', and a little later, 'It's myself I'm not too fond of'. This could be interpreted as a sign of alcoholism and the extent to which Frank might or might not be an alcoholic is an interesting one. In the strict medical sense of the term Frank is some way off suffering from alcoholism as an illness. He is certainly a hard drinker who can knock back the booze but on stage he remains articulate and entertaining. However he eventually goes several drinks too far and his employers are forced into finding the solution of him taking a sabbatical in Australia. Frank is fortunate that he is given some sort of reprieve because most employers would probably have given him the sack for professional misconduct.

As a teacher, Frank finds himself having to wrestle with the dilemma of knowing he has to discipline Rita's mind if she is to stand any chance of passing academic examinations. He is able to come up with a well-turned phrase which sums up his ironic view of education: 'We pluck birds from the sky and nail them down to learn how they fly.' In the process of teaching Rita the objectivism of literary criticism, there is a danger that her spontaneity and individualism may be lost. However, there are countless examples in the play when the boundaries between what should be a professional relationship between a lecturer and his student cross over into the realms of the personal and the private. To some extent, Frank's drunken state gives him licence to flirt with Rita and allows him to get away with mischievous comments such as 'Ah but Rita, if I was *yours* would I even consider stopping out for days?' or 'Right now there are a thousand things I'd rather do than teach – most of them with you young woman'. Equally though, Rita's strength of character in giving as good as she gets and her own inquisitiveness and ignorance of any social propriety, enables Frank to say such things without any fear of his inappropriate behaviour being reported to the authorities. It is evident with his other students, however, that they are not as forgiving or prepared to make the same kind of allowances as Rita and he is indignant when they justifiably complain about his drunken antics on the lecture stand.

The fact that Rita is unabashed at asking Frank questions about his personal life is the means by which more background information is gleaned about him. When Rita quite bluntly asks him if he is married, Frank is soon worn down by her persistence and the fact that she seems genuinely interested in him as a person. It does not take him long to tell her about this episode in his personal life.

> We split up Rita, because of poetry [. . .] One day . . . my then wife pointed out to me that for the preceding fifteen years my output as a poet had dealt exclusively with that brief period in which we had . . . *discovered* each other [. . .] and so, to give me something fresh to fire the muse, she left me. A very selfless and noble woman my ex-wife – she sacrificed her marriage for the sake of literature. (p. 24)

However disenchanted and disengaged with teaching Frank may have become, there is still plenty of evidence to suggest that he can do the job and do it well. One of the most laborious aspects of teaching is marking essays and yet time and again he is seen marking students' work and he is never late giving feedback to Rita. Despite Rita's best efforts to distract him, Frank does put his foot down on occasions and make her complete some written work. His brilliance as a teacher comes out when he uses Rita's description of her life at home to enable her to see a parallel with the situation in Forster's novel. Frank points out how she is able to make the connections in her own life that the characters in the novel cannot. He demonstrates how she will 'have a much better understanding of something if you discover it for yourself'.

As well as his academic role, Frank has also to take on a more pastoral one as he is party to the disintegration in Rita's marriage. His initial weariness and sarcasm about her persistent lateness and lack of work is transformed into understanding and shock as she relates the tale of Denny burning her books. When she arrives with her bag packed in the scene before the interval his reaction is to 'do a Rita' and use an expletive: 'ogh . . . fuck'. In the original version this line was written just as 'Tch' which was obviously not a strong enough reaction. Frank shows the sympathetic side of his character by suggesting that they cancel the tutorial and go and have a heart-to-heart in the pub, although he is probably as much in need of a drink as Rita is. For once he has to deal with real emotions and feelings and not those to be found in literature. For the first time Frank admits to her that he feels that she is 'good enough' to pass the course but that if he continues to teach her that she will no longer be the unique individual that she is: 'Rita, I don't know that I want to teach you. What you already have is valuable.'

For Frank, Act Two of the play is downhill all the way. Rita has found the intellectual confidence during the summer school that she lacked in the first half of the play and her abilities take flight while Frank is bent on committing professional suicide. While Rita has the last word in every scene in Act One (including Scene Three when Frank is reading her words), in Act Two, the situation is reversed and the ending of each scene focuses much more on Frank: this reinforces the change in status between the two characters. In Act Two, Scene One, Frank has taken up smoking again, has had 'a crap summer in France' and Julia has left him. Rita returns full of her exciting news of the summer school and her time in London. Frank's present to her of French cigarettes is now redundant as she has given up smoking and in contrast, she has bought him a pen that is only to be used for writing poetry. Rita's upbeat mood is the polar opposite of Frank's. When Rita sees the whisky bottle she says: 'Why d'y' do it when y've got so much goin' for y', Frank?' Frank's response is completely negative and he sees her leaving his company as inevitable: 'What do I do

when, in appalling sobriety, I watch you walk away and
disappear, your influence gone for ever?' The situation for
Frank worsens when he realises that his influence on Rita's
education is lessening. Contrary to his early description of
being able to 'nail her down to see how she flies', Rita has
soaked up the experience of the summer school and is
threatening to take flight quite independently of Frank.
Rita's association with the other students, especially Tyson,
sparks off a jealous reaction: 'Is there much point in working
towards an examination if you're going to fall in love and set
off for the South of [France] . . .?'

In the third scene of the second act, Frank is very drunk
and physically manoeuvres Rita into the chair because he is
almost resentful of the way she is beginning to express her
own views about a Blake poem that are contrary to his own.
He is also angry that he had to find out about her no longer
being a hairdresser by accident when she used to tell him
these personal details herself. Certain aspects of Rita's
private life have taken centre stage in Frank's imagination
and his reaction to things is out of all proportion to their
relative importance. Frank feels that Rita is slipping from his
grasp and his outlandish behaviour towards her threatens to
push her even further away. His drinking becomes even
heavier and the full extent of this is apparent in his
incoherent attempts at first phoning the bistro and then
Trish to get Rita to contact him about her examination. In
Scene Five he has the embittered arrogance to suggest that
in teaching Rita, like Mary Shelley's Frankenstein, he has
created a monster and ultimately he gets the reaction from
Rita that he deserves, which is that she slams the door in his
face.

The last scene of the play sees Frank packing his things
away and there is a glimmer of hope for him when he says,
'I hear good things about Australia.' In asking Rita if she
would go with him, he probably knows her answer already.
They have got this far together, but for the next stage of
their lives they need to go their separate ways. Frank has
helped Rita achieve her goal of passing her exams and in
the process he has discovered a lot about himself. Early on

in the play Rita says, 'I haven't bought myself a new dress
for the past twelve months. An' I'm not gonna get one
either; not till I pass my first exam. An' then I'll get a proper
dress, the sort of dress you'd only see on an educated
woman . . .' In giving Rita a dress as a gift at the end of the
play Frank is acknowledging that she is equal to any of the
educated women he has known and that deep down he has
always fancied her. In the closing moment of the play it is
Frank who receives our final attention as Rita takes her
scissors to his straggly hair and begins her physical attempt
to take ten years off him. This final action of the play
completes the circle of this episode in the lives of both the
characters and brings back echoes of Rita's speech from
early on in the drama:

> They walk into the hairdresser's and expect to walk out an
> hour later as a different person. I tell them, I'm just a
> hairdresser, not a plastic surgeon. See, most of them, that's
> why they come the hairdresser's – because they want to be
> changed. But if you wanna change y' have to do it from the
> inside, don't y'? Know like I'm doin' . . . tryin' to do. (p. 13)

By trimming Frank's hair, Rita can change his external
appearance but she cannot change the person inside, only
he can do that for himself. The coming of Rita into Frank's
life is the engine for change. She makes a point of telling
him in the final moments that he is a good teacher and that
he has given her the gift of education that will now enable
her to make a choice about her future. Rita has indeed
changed 'from the inside' and the question for Frank is
whether he is prepared and able to do the same.

The play's reception

The initial press reaction to *Educating Rita* was an almost
grudging acceptance of the fact it was a play likely to gain
immediate audience appeal. It was variously compared with
Shaw's *Pygmalion*, Wesker's *Roots*, Simon Gray's *Butley* and
Emlyn Williams's *The Corn is Green*. What these plays have in
common is that they all deal with a teacher/student

relationship or are about how education can improve an individual's position in life. Almost every first review of the play makes a connection between *Educating Rita* and *Pygmalion*.

> 'Treading eagerly in the upwardly mobile footsteps of Shaw's Eliza Doolittle . . .' (*Observer*, 22 June 1980)

> 'Like Eliza Doolittle, this particular applicant is spirited, lively and soon in charge of the situation.' (*Sunday Telegraph*, 22 June 1980)

> '*Educating Rita* . . . is so like *Pygmalion* in some ways that you half expect Rita to start trying out "The Rain in Spain Stays Mainly in the Plain".' (*Evening Standard*, 18 June 1980)

> 'With its echoes of *Pygmalion* . . .' (*Daily Telegraph*, 18 June 1980)

> 'Like *Roots* and *Pygmalion*, Willy Russell's *Educating Rita* is one of those plays in which a female pupil learns from and eventually outstrips her male teacher.' (*Guardian*, 17 June 1980)

Educating Rita has not only joined this list of literary works but has also become as popular as, if not more so than, any of them. Much has been made of the similarities between Eliza Doolittle in Shaw's play and Rita because they are both spirited characters from working-class backgrounds. Eliza's transformation is rooted in the prejudice that existed in Edwardian society against anyone who spoke with a regional accent. In Shaw's play, Eliza is passed off as someone from the upper classes by being taught society manners and etiquette and how to speak 'properly'. When Rita puts on a posh accent in one of Frank's tutorials, he thinks there is something wrong with her voice and asks her to stop it. Until the late 1960s, there were virtually no television or radio presenters on the BBC with a regional accent whereas now it is almost a requirement for the job. The irony is that while the critics were able to demonstrate their literary prowess by citing *Pygmalion* in their reviews as a probable model for *Educating Rita*, Willy Russell had never seen or read Shaw's play.

> I had heard of Shaw's play and the subsequent musical but had no particular familiarity with his plot or theme. Having

completed *Educating Rita* I located a copy of *Pygmalion* and
spent a satisfying hour or two reading Shaw's play. As I
suspected there was, for me, no similarity between the two
plays other than those of plot, i.e. teacher/pupil and class
divide.

  Since then, of course, critics right around the world have
usually mentioned *Pygmalion* in the same breath as *Educating
Rita*. Does it bother me to have *Pygmalion* mentioned so often in
the context of *Educating Rita*? Not one bit. To be mentioned in
the same breath as the old Irish rascal Shaw is always a
delight. (Russell in Sullivan, 1990, p. 2)

Another factor which operated against the play in the eyes
of the press was its opening at a venue associated with more
experimental and serious-minded work. The week after the
play opened and when all of the daily and Sunday
newspaper reviews had appeared, Sheridan Morley summed
up the initial critical reaction to the play in *Punch*:

What we have here is an eminently commercial two-character
comedy, better indeed than most comedies currently on offer
in the West End, which has nothing at all to do with the RSC
and still less to do with the experimental nature of the
Warehouse. Moreover there is a Pavlovian critical reflex
whereby a play opening at, say, the Fortune or the
Ambassadors is treated totally differently from a show opening
at the Warehouse, and had Mr Russell gone to either of the
former homes I suspect reaction to his play would have been a
great deal warmer. (25 June 1980)

The *Daily Telegraph* review is entitled 'Trash reader turning
to classics' and its author, Eric Shorter, more or less sets
about trashing the play itself.

Educating Rita seems under-dramatised and fitter perhaps for
the television screen [. . .] it seems too sketchy to merit two
hours of stage time, since it adds up to nothing more than a
series of interviews between a student and her teacher. The
contrast in their characters, ages and cultures makes them
amusing company – especially the student as played by Julie
Walters in a rich and reverberative Lancashire dialect [. . .] If
the evening is finally unsatisfactory it is perhaps because we
cannot see beyond the study (and the two-handed structure)
which forbids either character's background to come to life

and requires so many entrances from the delightful squeaky-voiced Miss Walters, reporting literary rather than dramatic progress. (18 June 1980)

The fact that this reviewer mistakes the Liverpudlian dialect for a Lancashire one only goes to illustrate the unfamiliarity of the London-based press at the time with any accent north of Watford. Michael Billington in the *Guardian*, while not glowing in his praise for the play, at least recognised the qualities that have assured its subsequent success:

> It suffers initially from a harvest of Liverpudlian corn but it grows into a touching and quite complex play about the melancholic way education often pulls people apart instead of pulling them together [. . .] With great particularity, Russell shows that education can be a joy (Rita takes to Shakespeare as a cat laps milk). But he also demonstrates that it means alienation from one's own background and also from one's mentor: a cosy dependence is replaced by the danger of solo flight. (17 June 1980)

The most promising review appeared in *The Times* and in it, Ned Chaillet predicted that the play was likely to attract the crowds once the word spread that the production provided an entertaining evening. Chaillet's one criticism of the play was that he felt that Willy Russell could have made more of the serious side of the drama rather than softening the subject matter by emphasising the comedic elements. In fact, Chaillet seems to be suggesting that it should be precisely the type of play that Willy Russell himself says that he does not write.

> What do I want to say? What moves me? What story do I want to tell? I believe that every play I have ever written has, ultimately, been one which celebrates the goodness of man; certainly, the plays have included emptiness, despair, possibly even baseness. But it is the goodness that I hope the audience is left with. I really don't want to write plays which are resigned, menopausal, despairing and whingeing. I don't want to use any medium as a platform for displaying the smallness and helplessness of man. Man is man because madly, possibly stupidly, but certainly wonderfully, he kicks against the inevitability of life. He spends his life looking for answers.

> There probably are no answers but the fact that man asks the
> questions is the reason I write plays. (Russell in K. A. Berney
> (ed.), *Contemporary British Dramatists*, St James' Press, 1994)

However, Chaillet is prepared to concede that 'the deft
moments of its best comedy are splendidly refreshing' and
he provides a perceptive summary of his overall impression
of the play's content and characters:

> Mr Russell has taken a look at two segments of English society
> and engineered a collision that is as full of regret as it is of
> promise [. . .] Miss Walters's breezy arrival, free of the ritual
> deference of usual students, briefly awakens a sense of moral
> pride in Frank. He values the rawness of her self-expression,
> and, although he is aghast at her ignorance, he immediately
> tries to step down as her tutor. What she wants to learn,
> however, she believes he can teach her; and the play goes
> forward by short scenes in the office as Rita challenges E.M.
> Forster and Peer Gynt with her plain-spoken Northern wit.
> (Ned Chaillet, *The Times*, 17 June 1980)

While the critics may have been divided in their opinions
regarding the relative merits of the play, there was almost
unanimous praise for Julie Walters's performance as Rita. In
1980, Julie Walters was not the household name she is today
and the role she created in *Educating Rita* (immortalised in
the film version) provided a significant turning point in her
career.

> A peach of a performance from Julie Walters who graduates
> from a chipper perkiness to a real self-awareness: an Eliza who
> would out-argue her Higgins rather than ever return to him.
> (Michael Billington, *Guardian*, 17 June 1980)

> Miss Walters is unmatched among young actresses at
> suggesting a mind chafing against restraints, and she has been
> developing, in addition to her native canniness, a joyously
> exuberant comic style [. . .] In this play, with due help from
> her author, she gathers more laughs in an evening than have
> been heard in the entire previous history of the Warehouse.
> But she is also moving, and – again with Mr Russell's
> assistance – she brings alive, through narrative, the whole
> history of her disintegrating marriage to a resentful husband:
> something not necessarily to be regretted, but still painful to go
> through. (Robert Cushman, *Observer*, 22 June 1980)

This last review is from a Sunday newspaper which is when the fortunes of the play suddenly turned around. In 1980, a journalist writing for a daily newspaper would have had to write his/her review as soon as the curtain came down on the press night and phone it in the same evening. With the press night for *Educating Rita* on a Monday, a critic writing for a Sunday newspaper had the relative luxury of time to think more about his/her review. On the strength of the reviews in the dailies, Willy Russell believed that the production would be short-lived and that interest in the play would fade away. However, John Peter's review in the *Sunday Times*, entitled 'Willy Russell: in a class of his own', changed all that and the rest, as they say, is history.

One way of describing Willy Russell's new play, *Educating Rita*, would be to say that it was about the meaning of education, which doesn't sound too exciting. Another would be to say that it is about the meaning of life. A third, that it is a cross between *Pygmalion* and *Lucky Jim*. A fourth, that it is simply a marvellous play, painfully funny and passionately serious; a hilarious social documentary; a fairy-tale with a quizzical, half-happy ending [. . .] Julie Walters takes the small stage like a frightened animal that carries its trap wherever it goes. Clad in shabby-glamorous clothes and sleek high boots, she strides gawkily about like a nervous, sexy flamingo and emits an elaborately appalling Liverpool-Irish accent which ought to be recorded for the benefit of twenty-first century folklorists. It is a devastating and warm-hearted performance; and as Rita graduates to boilersuits and plimsolls she also acquires the dubious treasure of second-hand opinion. Literature, from being an alien land, threatening, marvellous or full of crap, becomes an all too well-discovered country where the mind is comforted with well-placed allusions [. . .] But Russell isn't just taking a swipe at education. For Rita, to learn all this is Life; it is experience, which teaches her about other things: people, choices, values, meanings. She may have cluttered up her mind with bizarre intellectual paraphernalia, but in the process she's finding herself, just as Frank is losing himself in drink, idleness and self-pity. I think Russell is saying that education is a dangerous drug which can have beneficial side-effects on the right patient: a freewheeling, humane conclusion which will upset puritans, heavy academics and dogmatic

> liberals. It sent me out moved, excited and exhilarated:
> feelings which I'm anxious for my readers to share. (22 June
> 1980)

Audiences were indeed queuing outside the Warehouse and
after its short run there it transferred to the Piccadilly
Theatre for a long run. In January 1981, while the
RSC/Omega Stage production was still running in the West
End, Willy Russell was granted the rights to stage a new
production in Liverpool. One of the main reasons for
mounting this production was to help turn around the ailing
fortunes of the Liverpool Playhouse which was in danger of
closing. Co-directed with Pip Broughton, it starred William
Gaunt as Frank and Kate Fitzgerald as the first native
Liverpudlian-speaking Rita.

Having been a big hit the first time around, the Liverpool
Playhouse staged a twenty-first anniversary production of
Educating Rita in 2002. Directed by Glen Walford and
starring Kirkby-born Angela Clarke and Richard
O'Callaghan, using the revised version of the text, the
production was so successful when it opened in April that it
was revived for the autumn season the same year.

> Glen Walford's production [. . .] is a joy from beginning to
> end, and still leaves much to relish and reflect upon. Angela
> Clarke, striking looking and immediately engaging, makes a
> terrific Rita, ideally foiled by Richard O'Callaghan's alcoholic,
> laconic, slightly jaded lecturer. [. . .] I had forgotten just how
> funny Russell's script is. Rather than representing a tidal wave
> of self-advancement by way of belly-laughs, it conjures up a
> constant crescendo of character development, where the
> humour is itself the stumbling process of discovering and then
> refining the finer things of life. (Joe Riley, 'All Reet, A Real
> Treat', *Liverpool Echo*, 18 April 2002)

The 2003 revised version

When the play was revived at the Liverpool Playhouse in
2002, Willy Russell took the opportunity to revisit the text
and make some minor amendments. As he says in his note

to this new version, the changes to the original are relatively modest but there are cuts, amendments and rewrites that are of some significance. Most of the changes occur in Act One. After twenty years, fashions and institutions come and go and some of the jokes might well have been lost on a twenty-first-century audience, so these kinds of references have been cut or updated. Rita originally had a line in the first scene when she was talking about her customers wanting their hairstyles changed, 'It's worse when there's a fad on', and of course the fads she goes on to describe were just that. Similarly in Act Two, Scene Two, for example, instead of comparing Rita's posh talk to 'a Dalek', Willy Russell has changed it to 'a parrot'. By 2002, the BBC television character Dr Who and his robotic enemies, the staccato-speaking Daleks had passed into cult legend. It is typical of fashion that less than three years after Willy Russell's revision, the series would be revived and the evil sound of the Daleks become recognised by a whole new generation.

What follows are a few examples of how this version of the text compares with the original and what differences these changes make to the play.

Act One, Scene One: The original stage instruction for the actor, '*we should recognise the voice of a man who shifts a lot of booze*', when Frank speaks into the phone has been cut. He now starts the speech with a slurring of Julia's name, 'Julia, Juliaa!' This establishes the name of 'his darling' right at the start of the scene whereas in the original her name was not revealed until near the end of Scene Two.

Rita's reference to a pornographic magazine of the time, *Men Only,* has been changed to 'before they had their videos', making it a more generic remark. But this will inevitably date because no doubt the pornographic industry of the future will be making full use of the most current technology.

At the time the play was written E.M. Forster's homosexuality was not widely known and the additional dialogue about him being gay is a sign of how attitudes towards sexual orientation have changed.

It is interesting to note the change to the ending of this scene. In the original, Rita leaves the room shutting the door quietly behind her and after a pause, bursts straight back in. She walks over to Frank and is a lot more direct with him: 'Wait a minute, listen to me. Listen: I'm on this course, you are my teacher – an' you're gonna bleedin' well teach me.' Frank is so taken aback by her approach that he asks her for a cigarette and he starts smoking. In the revised version the effect is quite different as the argument is conducted either side of the door on which Rita is frantically knocking: '*it being* that *door it won't open again*'. Frank thinks he is safe for a moment until the door finally gives way.

Act One, Scene Two: The opening of this scene now has more extended stage business and establishes more clearly the fact that Frank is trying to resist the temptation to have a drink.

The missing scene: The scene that originally came next was cut when the first production moved into the West End, apparently to make the interval happen slightly earlier. It appears in the published edition of the play and picks up on Rita's attempt at writing an essay on *Howards End*, which she has tried to compare with a piece of 'pulp fiction'. It also makes clear that Frank has cut down on the booze. However, its removal pushes the action further on in time and gets us straight to the *Peer Gynt* essay.

Act One, Scene Three: Rita's speech at the beginning is entirely new and serves to provide a bit more background to her 'day job'. Willy Russell's fondness for alliteration, a stylistic feature of his novel, *The Wrong Boy*, is illustrated by the wonderful phrase, 'a Chinese chippie in Childwall'. The speech also gives us more information about the way in which Rita is juggling her job with getting to the university for around 5.30 or 6pm.

A significant piece of rewriting occurs when Rita

describes what she believes passes for working-class culture. In the original version she blames the tabloid press and the trade unions for encouraging people to make money in order to spend it. She equates materialism with a way of covering up all the ills in society and sees it as a replacement for understanding the real meaning of life. With hindsight, it is possible to recognise that during the Thatcher government of the 1980s, when people were encouraged to buy their council houses and the trade unions were crushed into near submission, this produced a generation greedy for material possessions. Willy Russell identifies it as the 'Got-to-Have game' which has as much resonance in contemporary British society as it does in the social context of the play's original period.

Act One, Scene Four: Frank's sarcasm over the lack of work from Rita is heightened in the revision with an additional line, the effect of which is to make him appear somewhat shamefaced when he learns that her essay and books have been burnt by Denny.

> Don't tell me! Last night, whilst you were asleep a couple of errant Oxbridge dons broke into your premises and appropriated your essay for their own highly dubious ends.

There is an interesting example in the scene of the altered line now creating an anachronism but it has been done to achieve what Willy Russell calls a way of enabling the play to be 'perceived as taking place in its own time'. It occurs when Rita talks about choice being between margarine and butter, which has been updated to 'He thinks we've *got* choice already because there's thirty-eight satellite channels to watch'.

Act One, Scene Five: It is now made clear that the book Frank is reading is a copy of *Rubyfruit Jungle*.

Act One, Scene Six: Originally, there was a stage direction which has Rita sharpening pencils while Frank berates her for not turning up at the dinner party. In the revised version she is just sitting.

Rita's description of herself as a 'half-caste' has been amended to 'I'm an alien'. Sociologically this is an interesting example of how language changes and how a term like 'half-caste' which was in common usage to describe someone of mixed race in the 1980s is now considered to be offensive.

Act Two: The reference to the fact that Frank is typing poetry and chain-smoking as he works at the start of the second half has now been removed. This may indicate that having Frank return to his muse was not a helpful suggestion to the actor. In Scene Three Rita's comparison between Somerset Maugham and Harold Robbins no longer makes sense with the excision of the original Act One, Scene Three, when they were first mentioned, so this has been changed to Thomas Hardy and Rita Mae Brown. The addition of Frank repeating the name 'Virginia' at the end of Scene Five creates a moment which allows his anger to subside and emphasises the fact that he has probably gone too far. In Scene Seven, there are two pieces of historical detail which have been cut. After Frank has asked Rita if she would like to go to Australia with him, he originally said 'It'd be good for us to leave a place that's just finishing for one that's just beginning.' Without this line, it is not clear what Rita means when she says, 'Isn't that called jumpin' a sinkin' ship?' In the late 1970s/early 1980s, especially in cities like Liverpool, unemployment was running at an all-time high and there was a strong sense that the country was in serious decline. For some the only hope for a prosperous life was to emigrate to places like Australia. Instead of saying, 'Ey, Frank, what's it like havin' your own bottle bank?', Rita originally said, 'Ey, Frank, if there was threepence back on each of those bottles you could buy Australia.' At the time the play was written most drink manufacturers charged a deposit on their bottles which was refundable upon return of the empties. With the need to recycle glass, this practice might well come back into use and the original line would once again have relevance to a contemporary audience.

The film version

When the director and producer, Lewis Gilbert, saw the stage production of *Educating Rita* he realised its potential as a film. The story of *Educating Rita* need not be a two-hander set in one location since it contains a host of other characters and situations which could be 'opened out' for movie purposes. Before writing the screenplay, Willy Russell had already had considerable experience and success at writing for television and he was well tuned to the more detailed and visual requirements of the recorded medium. However, this was the first time he had adapted his own work for the screen and he worked collaboratively with Lewis Gilbert in deciding the content and structure of the film version. The film script retains almost all of the scenes from the stage version but there is a considerable amount of new material and less than half of the original dialogue.

Though the main focus of the film is still on the Frank/Rita relationship through their tutorials, it now extends to include scenes of both Rita and Frank at home and at work. The cast list contains twenty-seven named roles, including a new character called Brian who is a colleague of Frank's, and there are new scenes with Denny and Trish. In the play, we only know Frank by his first name, but in the course of the film we learn that professionally his title is Dr Bryant. There are also some entirely new situations created for the film, for example, a comic sub-plot involving Brian having an affair with Frank's partner, Julia. Whenever Frank walks into a scene that involves Julia and Brian, Brian picks up a phone and pretends to be talking to his publisher. This running gag culminates in Brian doing it once too often and Frank revealing that he knows about the affair by pointing out that the phone has been cut off. Rita is shown at home with Denny who is demolishing a wall while she is trying to study upstairs. The trigger for Denny burning her books is when he finds Rita's contraceptive pills hidden under a loose floorboard.

One of the most important crossovers from stage to screen is the retention of Julie Walters in the title role but in order to secure the finance for the film, it needed a well-known film star like Michael Caine to be cast as Frank. Caine's fee for the film was reportedly a quarter of the four-million-pound budget and one of the reasons why the film was made in Dublin and not Liverpool was because he was a UK tax exile at the time. Caine had previously been directed by Lewis Gilbert in the successful 1966 film *Alfie* and he was attracted to *Educating Rita* because 'there was a technical aspect about the difference between theatre and film acting that was also to my advantage in making any impression in a play that was so obviously a vehicle for the female lead. In the play, Rita does all the moving about on the stage, while the man, for most of the time, just sits at his desk and listens and reacts. Now the theatre is about "acting"; the cinema is about "reacting". When Rita said something, the camera had to cut to me for my reaction. You can't do that on stage, and that is what helped to balance the weight of the two parts in the film and made it acceptable to me' (Caine, 1992, p. 397).

Partly because the film was shot mostly on location in and around Dublin during the summer months, it has a different time-line to the play. The film starts in the summer because the sun is shining and the leaves are on the trees. Rita's sister's wedding takes place outside a church when there is snow on the ground and there is still snow on the university steps when Rita goes to see Frank after she has left Denny. This is the scene which is equivalent to the one that takes place at the end of Act One in the play. In the film version there is quite a time-lapse at this point because it cuts to Frank seeing Rita off on a train to go to the summer school. Autumn is suggested by a close-up of a tree branch without its leaves and by rain, but as an item of film continuity trivia, it is still possible to see the leaves on the trees outside the window in the subsequent scene when Rita is in the study trying to talk posh. With a close-up of blossom on a tree, there is a change to spring in the next scene when Rita is involved in a discussion on D. H. Lawrence with Tiger and some other students on the lawn. In the stage version Rita's examination takes place near the end of the autumn term and she bids Frank farewell just before Christmas. The final scenes in the film take place at the end of the summer term. The film does not set out to improve upon the play but to tell Rita's story differently and in a way that suits the medium and resources of film. For example, when Frank is looking for his bottle of whisky in the first scene, the camera pans along the editions of Gibbon, Wilde, Chaucer, Shakespeare and Milton and stops at a copy of a novel by Charles Jackson called *The Lost Weekend*, behind which Frank has concealed a bottle of Black-and-White whisky. This kind of visual referencing to a novel about an alcoholic can only work on film.

The music for the film was composed, performed and produced by David Hentschel who had worked on two previous films with Lewis Gilbert. David Hentschel is well known in the popular music world, having started his career as a sound engineer on classic albums such as Elton John's *Goodbye Yellow Brick Road*. The score is written for synthesisers with saxophone and guitars, giving it a contemporary feel. There are three major themes to the soundtrack, one for Rita, one for Frank and one that conveys the world of academia. The latter sounds like a piece of synthesised J. S. Bach, which suggests an interesting mix of the traditional and the modern. Rita's theme is a tuneful melody that starts with a falling interval and has an optimistic feel about it. Frank's theme is much more turbulent with a march-like accompaniment and a rising minor third interval that gives it quite a melancholic feel.

The film proved to be extremely popular, as illustrated in this review for a repeat showing on television:

> This comedy drama is a joy from start to finish, largely thanks
> to Willy Russell's crisp adaptation of his hugely successful
> stage play and the lead actors' divine suitability for their roles.
> Julie Walters (in her feature film debut) is great as the sassy,
> streetwise heroine who's eager for higher learning but smart

enough to spot the foibles of her boozy tutor at a hundred paces. Meanwhile, Michael Caine has one of his best ever roles as the drink-sodden, cynical lecturer who's on his own road to enlightenment, a performance that garnered his most favourable notice in years. There were some who moaned at the time that Walters's portrayal patronised bright working-class girls, but she brings genuine warmth to the part and, like Caine, deservedly received a BAFTA statuette and an Academy Award nomination. (Sue Heal, *Radio Times*, 21 December 2006)

Further Reading

Brown, Rita Mae, *Rubyfruit Jungle*, Bantam Books, 1977

Caine, Michael, *What's It All About*, Century, 1992

Gill, John, *Willy Russell and his Plays*, Countyvise Publications, 1992

Kinsman, Rob, *Face to Face with Willy Russell*, 2004, www.queens-theatre.co.uk

McCarthy, Shaun, *Creative Lives: Willy Russell*, Heinemann, 2002

Russell, Willy, *Educating Rita* with additional material, ed. Albert-Reiner Glaap, Verlag Moritz Diesterweg, 1997

——, *Plays: 1* (contains *Breezeblock Park, Our Day Out, Stags and Hens* and *Educating Rita*), with an introduction by the author, Methuen, 1996

——, *Blood Brothers*, Methuen Drama Student Edition, Methuen, 1995

——, *Shirley Valentine and One for the Road*, Methuen, 1993

——, *The Wrong Boy*, Doubleday, 2000

——, 'Letter to a BBC Producer' (1984), in K.A. Berney (ed.), *Contemporary British Dramatists*, St James's Press, 1994

——, foreword in James Pye, *Second Chances: Adults Returning to Education*, Oxford University Press, 1991

Sullivan, Theresa, *Educating Rita*, Longmans Literature Guidelines, Longman, 1990

Website: www.willyrussell.com

Educating Rita (DVD), directed by Lewis Gilbert, Carlton Visual Entertainment

Hoovering the Moon (CD), WR Records, 2003

Works on similar themes

Amis, Kingsley, *Lucky Jim*, Penguin, 1961

Gray, Simon, *Butley*, in Gray: *Key Plays*, Faber, 2002

Heller, Zoë, *Notes on a Scandal*, Penguin, 2004

Mamet, David, *Oleanna*, Methuen Drama Student Edition, Methuen, 2004

Potter, Dennis, *The Nigel Barton Plays*, Penguin Plays, 1967

Shaw, George Bernard, *Pygmalion*, Penguin Plays, 1941

Wesker, Arnold, *Roots*, in Wesker: *Plays 1*, Methuen, 2001

Williams, Emlyn, *The Corn is Green*, Samuel French, 1995

Educating Rita

Educating the author

I was born in Whiston, which is just outside Liverpool. They talk funny in Whiston. To a Liverpudlian everyone else talks funny. Fortunately, when I was five my mum and dad moved to Knowsley, into an estate full of Liverpudlians who taught me how to talk correctly.

My dad worked in a factory (later, having come to hate factory life, he got out and bought a chip shop) and my mother worked in a warehouse; in those days there was a common ritual called employment. I went to school just down the road from my grandma's mobile grocer's (it was in an old charabanc which had long since lost any chance of going anywhere but everyone called it the mobile).

In school I learned how to read very early. Apart from reading books I played football and kick-the-can and quite enjoyed the twice-weekly gardening lessons. We each had a plot and at the end of the summer term we could take home our turnips and lettuces and radish and stuff. We used to eat it on the way. Our headmaster (Pop Chandler) had a war wound in his leg and everyone said it was 'cos of the shrapnel. When we went to the baths (if he was in a good mood) he'd show us this hole in his leg. It was horrible. It was blue. We loved looking at it.

Other than reading books, gardening, playing football and looking at shrapnel wounds I didn't care much for school. I watched the telly a lot. Never went to any theatres or anything like that. Saw a show at the village hall once but it was all false. They talked funny and got married at the end. I only remember it 'cos I won the raffle, a box of fruit, with a coconut right in the middle. When we opened it the coconut stank. It was bad.

When I was eleven they sent me to a secondary school in Huyton. Like all the other Knowsley kids I was frightened of Huyton. There were millions of new houses there and flats, and everyone said there were gangs with bike chains and broken bottles and truck spanners. What everyone said was right; playtime was nothing to do with play, it was about survival. Thugs roamed the concrete and casually destroyed

anything that couldn't move fast enough. Dinner time was
the same only four times as long.

If you were lucky enough to survive the food itself you
then had to get out into the playground world of protection
rackets, tobacco hustlers, trainee contract killers and plain
no-nonsense sadists. And that's without the teachers!

Anders his name was, the metalwork teacher. All the
other kids loved metalwork. First thing we had to do was file
a small rectangle of metal so that all the sides were straight;
this would then be name-stamped and used as a nameplate
to identify each kid's work. I never completed mine. After a
matter of weeks other kids had moved from making
nameplates to producing anything from guns and daggers to
boiler-room engines while it was obvious that I was never
going to be able to get the sides of my piece of metal
straight. Eventually it was just a sliver, a near-perfect needle,
though not straight. I showed it to him, Anders; I couldn't
hide it from him any longer. He chucked it in the bin and
wordlessly handed me another chunk of metal and indicated
that I had to do it again and again and again until I did it
right! And I did, for a whole school year, every metalwork
lesson, tried and failed and with every failure there came a
chunk of metal and the instruction to do it again. I started to
have terrible nightmares about Anders. It's the only time I
can remember feeling real hatred for another human being.

After another year I moved schools, to Rainford where it
used to be countryside, where they all talked funny, where
the thugs were rather old-fashioned, charming even.
Whereas in Huyton you could be bike-chained to bits
without warning, in Rainford the thugs observed some sort
of manners: 'Ey you, does t' want t' fight wi me?' You could
still get hurt, of course, and some of the teachers were
headcases; but there were no sadists, metalwork was not on
the curriculum, there were fields and lawns in place of
concrete playgrounds and compared to Huyton it was
paradise. We even had a long lesson every week called
'silent reading'; just enter the classroom and pick up a book,
start reading and as long as you made no noise you were left
completely alone with your book. I remember clearly,

during one of these lessons, locked into a novel, the sun streaming through the windows, experiencing the feeling of total peace and security and thinking what a great thing it must be to write books and create in people the sort of feeling the author had created in me. I wanted to be a writer!

It was a wonderful and terrible thought – wonderful because I sensed, I knew, it was the only thing for me. Terrible because how could I, a kid from the 'D' stream, a piece of factory fodder, ever change the course that my life was already set upon? How the hell could I ever be the sort of person who could become a writer? It was a shocking and ludicrous thought, one that I hid deep in myself for years, but one that would not go away.

During my last year at school they took us to a bottle-making factory in St Helens, me and all the other kids who were obviously factory types. I could feel the brutality of the place even before I entered its windowless walls. Inside, the din and the smell were overpowering. Human beings worked in there but the figures I saw, feeding huge and relentlessly hungry machines, seemed not to be a part of humanity but a part of the machinery itself. Those men who were fortunate enough to not have to work directly with the machinery, the supervisors, foremen I suppose, glared, prodded, occasionally shouted. Each one of them looked like Anders from the metalwork class.

Most of the kids with whom I visited that place accepted that it was their lot to end up in that place. Some even talked of the money they would earn and made out that they couldn't wait to get inside those walls.

But in truth, I think they all dreaded it as much as I. Back in school I stared at the geography books I hadn't read, the history pages and science I hadn't studied, the maths books (which would still be a mystery today, even if I'd studied them from birth), and I realised that with only six months' schooling to go, I'd left it all hopelessly too late. Like it or not I'd end up in a factory. There was no point in trying to catch up with years of schoolwork in a mere six months. And so I didn't. The months I had left were spent sagging

school and going to a dark underground club every
lunchtime. It was called the Cavern and the smell of sweat
in there was as pungent as any in a factory, the din was
louder than any made by machines. But the sweat was
mingled with cheap perfume and was produced by dancing
and the noise was music, made by a group called the
Beatles.

One afternoon in summer I left the Cavern after the
lunchtime session and had to go to the Bluecoat Chambers
to sit an examination, the result of which would determine
how suited I was to become an apprentice printer. I didn't
want to be an apprentice printer; I wanted to be back in the
Cavern. I did the exam because my dad thought it would be
a good thing. I answered the questions on how many men it
would take to lift three tons of coal on a rainy day etc. And I
wrote the essay of my choice (titled 'A Group Called The
Beatles'). And I failed.

At home there were conferences, discussions, rows and
slanging matches all on the same subject – me and the job
I'd get. Eventually my mother resolved it all. She suggested
I become a ladies' hairdresser! I can only think that a desire
to have her hair done free must have clouded her normally
reasonable mind. It was such a bizarre suggestion that I
went along with it. I went to a college for a year or so and
pretended to learn all about hairdressing. In reality most of
my time was spent at parties or arranging parties. It was a
good year but when it ended I had to go to work. Someone
was actually prepared to hire me as a hairdresser, to let me
loose on the heads of innocent and unsuspecting customers.
There were heads scalded during shampooing, heads which
should have become blonde but turned out green, heads of
Afro frizz (before Afro frizz had been invented) and heads
rendered temporarily bald. Somehow, probably from
moving from one shop to another before my legendary
abilities were known, I survived. For six years I did a job I
didn't understand and didn't like. Eventually I even had my
own small salon and it was there that on slack days I would
retire to the back room and try to do the one and only thing
I felt I understood, felt that I could do: write.

I wrote songs mostly but tried, as well, to write sketches and poetry, even a book. But I kept getting interrupted by women who, reasonably enough on their part, wanted their hair done. It dawned upon me that if ever I was to become a writer I had first to get myself into the sort of world which allowed for, possibly even encouraged such aspiration. But that would mean a drastic change of course. Could I do it? Could I do something which those around me didn't understand? I would have to break away. People would be puzzled and hurt. I compromised. I sensed that the world in which I would be able to write would be the academic world. Students have long holidays. I'd be able to spend a good part of the year writing and the other part learning to do a job, teaching perhaps, which would pay the rent. I wasn't qualified to train as a teacher but I decided to dip my toe in the water and test the temperature. I enrolled in a night class for O level English Literature and passed it. To go to a college though, I'd need at least five O levels. Taking them at night school would take too long. I had to find a college which would let me take a full-time course, pack everything into one year. I found a college but no authority was prepared to give me a maintenance grant or even pay my fees. I knew I couldn't let the course go, knew I could survive from day to day – but how was I going to find the money to pay the fees? The hairdressing paid nothing worth talking of.

I heard of a job, a contract job in Fords, cleaning oil from the girders high above the machinery. With no safety equipment whatsoever and with oil on every girder the danger was obvious. But the money was big.

I packed up the hairdresser's and joined the night-shift girder cleaners. Some of them fell and were injured, some of them took just one look at the job and walked away. Eventually there were just a few of us desperate or daft enough to take a chance.

I stayed in that factory just long enough to earn the fees I needed; no extras, nothing. Once I'd earned enough for the fees, I came down from the girders, collected my money and walked away. I enrolled at the college and one day in

September made my way along the stone-walled drive. The obvious difference in age between me and the sixteen-year-olds pouring down the drive made me feel exposed and nervous but as I entered the glass doors of Childwall College I felt as if I'd made it back to the beginning. I could start again. I felt at home.

Willy Russell

Author's note to the revised edition

Whilst I realise that the text of *Educating Rita* is frequently prescribed for examinations and I would not want to override the needs of students and their examiners (and indeed will do whatever I can to accommodate them) my main consideration is with the companies that act my plays and the audiences that watch them. And it is for this reason that I would like to make available this updated version of *Rita*. I haven't, in any way, radically overhauled the text to the extent of changing the play itself. What I have done (and what proved to be enormously successful on the two occasions we produced it here in Liverpool in 2002) is to address those areas where there were very, very specific references to the time in which the play was originally written. Whilst I have not tried to reset the play in the twenty-first century, what I have done is cut and edit and rewrite in such a way that the play *can* be perceived as taking place in its own time (something that just wasn't possible when the text contained references to figures and institutions and attitudes firmly of the late 1970s/early 1980s). I'm convinced that, for any company, this version would be something of a bonus.

This revised text is set from the prompt copy of 2002's Liverpool Playhouse production.

Willy Russell
March 2003

Educating Rita was first performed on 10 June 1980 at the Royal Shakespeare Company Warehouse, London, with the following cast:

Frank   Mark Kingston
Rita   Julie Walters

Directed by Mike Ockrent
Designed by Poppy Mitchell

Educating Rita subsequently transferred to the Piccadilly Theatre, London, and the cast changed several times during a long run.

It was also filmed with Michael Caine as Frank and Julie Walters as Rita directed by Lewis Gilbert.

Act One

Scene One

A book-lined tutorial room on the first floor of a Victorian-built university in the north of England.

There is a large bay window with a desk placed in front of it. There is also another desk or table covered with various books and papers. On one wall there hangs a good and striking print of a nude, religious scene.

Frank, *who is in his early fifties, is standing holding an empty mug whilst pondering his shelves.*

Frank Now where in the name of God . . . Eliot, Eliot . . .? (*He goes to one of the bookshelves and starts to remove books. He is puzzled.*) Eliot? Emerson? E, E, E, Euripides . . . (*With sudden enlightenment.*) Ah! Eureka, D, D, D, D, Dickens! (*He replaces books and moves to another section of shelving jubilantly removing a couple of Dickensian tomes.*) One can always rely on Dickens. (*He lifts out the books to reveal the bottle of scotch which has no more than about three or four fingers left in it; this he pours into his mug which he then raises in salute.*) To my dear Charlie Dickens, genius and keeper of the scotch. (*He raises the mug to drink.*)

The phone rings, startling him slightly. Hurriedly he replaces the now empty bottle and the books before taking a gulp of the scotch and answering the phone.

Julia, Juliaa! . . . Well yes, obviously I'm still here . . . Because I've got this Open University woman coming this evening, haven't I? . . . Tch . . . Darling, I did tell you, of course I did . . . Well, then you shouldn't have prepared supper, should you? Because I said, darling, I distinctly recall saying that I would be late . . . Yes, yes, I probably *shall* go to the pub afterwards – I shall no doubt *need* to go to the pub afterwards if only to mercifully wash away some silly woman's attempts to get into the mind of Henry James or Thomas Hardy or whoever the hell it is we're supposed to study on this course . . . Christ, why did I take this on?

. . . Yes, darling, yes, I suppose I did take it on to pay for the drink . . . Oh, for God's sake, just leave it in the oven . . . Julia, if you're trying to induce feelings of guilt at the prospect of a charred dinner you'd have been better cooking something other than lamb and ratatouille . . . Because, my perfect poppet, I like my lamb cooked to the point of abuse and even a culinary ignoramus such as I knows that ratatouille is a dish that is impossible to overcook . . . Darling, you could incinerate ratatouille, radiate it, cook it in the ovens of hell, napalm the bloody stuff and still it wouldn't be overcooked! . . . Determined to go to the pub? When did I need determination to get *me* into a pub . . .?

There is a knock at the door.

Look, I'll have to go . . . there's someone at the door . . . Yes, yes . . . I . . . all right, I promise . . . just a couple of pints . . . (*Sotto voce.*) four . . .!

Further, more insistent knocking at the door.

(*Calling in the direction of the door.*) Come in! (*He continues into the phone.*) Yes, I prom— all right . . . yes, yes!

More knocking from the door.

Come in! (*Into the phone.*) Absolutely, darling, absolutely . . . yes . . . bye-bye . . . (*He replaces the receiver.*) Come in! COME IN!

The door swings open, revealing **Rita**.

Rita   I *am* comin' in, aren't I? It's that stupid bleeding handle on the door. Y' wanna get it fixed!

Frank   Erm, yes. I erm . . . I er . . . I suppose I always meant to.

Rita   Well, that's no good, always meaning to, is it? Y' should get on with it. Because one of these days you'll be shouting 'come in' and it'll go on for ever and ever because the poor bastard on the other side of the door won't be able to come in. An' you won't be able to get out!

Frank   Now, you are?

Rita   What am I?

Frank   Pardon?

Rita   What?

Frank (*prompting her now*)   You are?

Rita   I'm a what?

Frank *busies himself with the papers on his desk.* **Rita** *is looking at the nude print. She becomes aware that* **Frank** *is watching her.*

Rita   It's nice, isn't it? The picture, it's nice.

Frank   Erm, yes, yes . . . I suppose it is, erm 'nice'.

Rita   It's very erotic.

Frank   Erm, well, I . . . you know, I don't think I've actually really looked at it for the past ten years or so (*He switches the picture light on.*) but . . . yes, I suppose it is.

Rita   There's no suppose about it – look at those tits.

Frank *again busies himself with the papers on his desk.*

Rita   Is it supposed to be erotic? (*She's being quite genuine here – truly believing that those she regards as 'educated people' can and do converse in such a way.*) Like, when he painted it, do y' think he like, like meant it to be a turn on, y' know, sexually stimulating?

Frank (*fascinated as much as he is fazed by her*)   Erm . . . probably . . .

Rita   I think he did, y' know. You don't paint pictures like that just so that people can admire the brush strokes, do y'?

Frank (*amused*)   No. No, you're probably right.

Rita   Because this was like the porn of its day, wasn't it? Y' know, before they had the videos; so this . . . this is the sort of thing they would have perved over in those days, isn't it? But back then they had to pretend there was nothing erotic about it at all so that's why they made it religious, didn't they? Do you think it's erotic?

Frank   I think it's very beautiful.

Rita   I didn't ask you if it was beautiful.

Frank   No. I know. But the term 'beautiful' covers the many feelings I have about the picture; including the feeling that yes, it is really rather erotic. (*He switches off the picture light.*)

Rita   D' y' get a lot like me?

Frank   I beg your pardon?

Rita   Do you get a lot of students like me?

Frank   Not exactly, no.

Rita   I was dead surprised when they accepted me. But I don't suppose they would have done if it had been a proper university, would they? It's different though, isn't it, the Open University? I suppose anyone can get in, can't they? D' y' think they must be desperate?

Frank   I . . . really couldn't say. I've not had much more experience of it than you have. In fact this is the first Open University work I've done.

Rita   Oh, great! I end up with a beginner!

Frank   No no, you misunderstand me; I work here at the university – I was just making the point that I haven't done this kind of extracurricular Open University work before.

Rita   It was a joke!

Frank   I am a bona fide lecturer but with . . .

Rita   A joke!

A beat.

Frank   Oh, I'm sorry. Yes, of course, 'a beginner', yes . . . (*He laughs now.*)

Rita   Quick? He's like lightnin'! So what y' doin' this for?
D' y' need the money?

Frank   Actually I do as a matter of fact.

Rita   Oh.

Frank   Erm . . . would you like to sit down?

Rita   No. Can I smoke?

Frank   Tobacco?

Rita   What?

Frank (*almost bashful*)   A joke.

Rita (*not quite sure for a second*)   Ogh. You mean was I gonna
whip out the wacky-backy? I hate drugs. They just cover
everything up. I hate them.

She produces a packet of cigarettes and offers one to **Frank**.

Frank (*hands aloft as if trying to physically ward off the temptation*)
Ah ah . . . I'd love one.

Rita   Well, have one!

Frank   No, no really, I've given up.

Rita   Everyone has. They're all afraid of gettin' cancer.
But they're all cowards. You've got to challenge death an'
disease. I read this great poem about fightin' death . . .

Frank   Ah, Dylan Thomas.

Rita   No, Roger McGough! It was all about this old man
who runs away from hospital and goes out on the ale. He
gets pissed and stands in the street shoutin' an' challengin'
death to come out an' fight. It's brilliant.

Frank   Mm. I don't think I'm familiar with the actual
piece you mean.

Rita   I'll bring y' the book; it's fantastic.

Frank   Good, good. That's very kind of you.

Rita   Mind you, you probably won't think it's any good at all.

Frank   Why not?

Rita   Because it's the sort of poetry you can understand.

Frank (*not quite sure*)   Ah. Yes. I see. So you think it's important then, that poetry should be understood?

Rita (*shrugging*)   Yeh. That's part of the reason I came here. Because there's loads that I don't understand.

Frank   You mean poetry? A lot of poetry you don't understand?

Rita (*beginning to move around and scan the books on the shelves*) Yeh. All kinds of things.

Frank (*watching her for a second or two*)   Look, can I offer you a drink?

Rita   What of?

Frank   Scotch?

Rita   You should be careful with that stuff; it kills your brain cells, y' know.

Frank   But you'll have one?

Rita (*going to the bookcase*)   Yeh. All right. It'll probably have a job even finding my brain . . .

Frank (*scratching his head as he ponders the bookshelves, thinking out loud*)   Now now now . . . thinks, thinks . . . F, F, F, Faulkner, Fielding . . . ah, Forster . . . Forster!

As he pulls away a couple of volumes of Forster, leaving them on the table desk, he reaches in and takes out another bottle of scotch which he then takes across to the small table.

Rita *is silently gobsmacked for a second.*

Rita   My aunty's got a drinks cabinet like that!

Frank   Water?

Rita No, I'll have the whisky. (*She picks up one of the Forster volumes.*) What's this like?

Frank (*bringing the drinks across and looking at the book*) *Howards End?*

Rita Yeh. Sounds filthy, doesn't it? E.M. Foster.

Frank Forster!

Rita Forced her to do what?

Frank (*watching her for a second before breaking into real and appreciative laughter*) Forster, E.M. Forster; and it's doubtful that he would have forced 'her' to do anything. Forster was a committed homosexual.

Rita Was he? Oh? So is that what his book's about, being gay?

Frank No, not at all. Actually it's about – but look, here . . . (*He hands her the book.*) Borrow it. Read it for yourself.

Rita OK. Thanks. I'll look after it. If I pack the course in I'll post it back to y'.

Frank Pack it in? You've not even started yet. Why should you pack it in?

Rita I don't know. I just might. Might decide it was a stupid idea.

Frank If you're already contemplating the possibility of 'packing it in', then why did you enrol in the first place?

Rita Because I want to know.

Frank *What?* What do you want to know?

Rita Everything.

Frank Everything? That's rather a lot, isn't it? Where were you thinking of beginning?

Rita Well . . . I'm a student now, aren't I? I'll have exams to do, won't I?

Frank   Well, yes, eventually.

Rita   So I'll have to learn about it all, won't I? It's like, y' sit there, don't y' – watchin' something like the ballet or the opera on the telly – an' y' just, y' know, call it rubbish because that's what it looks like, because y' don't understand – y' don't know how to see it – so y' just switch over or switch off an' say, 'that's fuckin' rubbish'.

Frank   You do?

Rita   Yeh. But I don't want to. Because I want to be able to see it. An' understand. Do you mind me swearin'?

Frank   No, not at all.

Rita   Do you swear?

Frank   When I need to, yes, of course. I've never subscribed to the idea that there's such a thing as bad language – only bad *use* of language.

Rita   See, the properly educated, they know it's only words, don't they? It's only the masses who don't understand. But that's because they're ignorant; it's not their fault, I know that, but sometimes they drive me mental. I do it to shock them sometimes; y' know if I'm in the hairdresser's – that's where I work – I'll say somethin' like 'I'm as fucked as a fanny on a Friday night!' and some of the customers, they'll have a right gob on them just 'cos I come out with something like that.

Frank   Yes, but in the circumstances that's hardly . . .

Rita   But it doesn't cause any kind of fuss with educated people though, does it? Because they know it's only words and they don't worry. But these stuck-up ones I meet, they think they're royalty just because they don't swear. An' anyway, I wouldn't mind but it's the aristocracy who swear more than anyone, isn't it, they're effing and blinding all day long; with them it's all, 'I say, the grouse is particularly fucking lovely today although I'm afraid the spuds are a bit bollocks, don't you think?' (*She sighs.*) But y' can't tell them that round our way. It's not their fault; they can't help it. But sometimes I hate them. (*Beat.*) God . . . what's it like to be free?

Frank   Ah, now there's a question. Another drink?

Rita (*shaking her head*)   Know if I'd got some other tutor I wouldn't have stayed.

Frank (*pouring himself another*)   What do you mean, another tutor?

Rita   Y' know, someone who objected to swearin'.

Frank   How did you know that I wouldn't object?

Rita   I didn't. I was just testin' y'.

Frank   Yes! You're doing rather a lot of that, aren't you?

Rita   I can't help it. That's what I do – y' know when I'm nervous.

Frank   And how am I doing so far?

Rita (*with a noncommittal shrug; crossing to the window*)   I love this room . . . this window. Do you like it?

Frank   What, the window?

Rita   Yeh.

Frank   It's not really something I consider, apart from those occasions when I feel an overwhelming urge to throw something through it.

Rita   Like what?

Frank   Oh, a student usually!

Rita (*amused*)   You're bleedin' mad you, aren't y'?

Frank   Quite possibly.

Beat.

Rita   Aren't you supposed to be interviewin' me?

Frank   Do I need to?

Rita   I know! I talk too much, don't I? I don't when I'm at home; I hardly ever talk at all when I'm there. But I don't often get the chance to talk to someone like you. Just tell me to shut up if I go on too much.

Frank   I wouldn't dream of telling you to 'shut up'.

Rita   What does 'assonance' mean?

Frank (*laughing and spluttering his drink*)   What the . . .

Rita   Don't laugh at me.

Frank (*hearing the tone and knowing he's touched a nerve; quickly recovering*)   No. No. Erm . . . I didn't mean . . . 'Assonance'. Well, it's, erm, it's a form of rhyme in which the corresponding vowels have the same sound but not the consonants that precede or follow the vowels. Now this can be slightly confusing because assonance can also be the use of identical consonants but with different vowels: erm, 'killed/cold' . . . 'draught/drift', 'pin/pan', 'gloom/gleam', 'drink/drank' . . .

Rita (*involuntarily*)   'Wink/wank'. (*She clasps a hand to her offending mouth.*)

Frank (*delighted she's grasped it*)   Yes, yes . . . that's right, that's right. Look, do you know Yeats?

Rita   The wine lodge?

Frank (*taking down a book from his shelves*)   The poet! W.B. Yeats, Irish poet. Look, you see, here . . . (*He shows her the relevant poem.*) 'The Wild Swans at Coole' and here, you see, see how he's using really subtle assonance, rhyming the word 'swan' with the word 'stone'.

Rita   So . . . so 'assonance' means gettin' the rhyme wrong?

Frank (*laughing in appreciation*)   Well, yes . . . yes, in a way, yes it does, it bloody well does, it means, 'getting the rhyme wrong', but deliberately, purposefully in order to achieve a certain lyrical, almost musical effect.

Rita   Oh. (*She sighs.*) There's loads I don't know.

Frank   Well, erm . . . It's Mrs White, is it?

She nods.

Frank   But would you mind if I called you by your name, your first name?

Rita   No.

Frank   So what is it?

Rita   My name? Oh, Rita.

Frank (*surprised; moving towards his desk*)   Rita?

Rita   Yeh.

Frank (*alluding to the papers on his desk*)   But it says here Mrs 'S.' White.

Rita   Oh that! Yeh, that's just 'S' for 'Susan'. That's my real name. I've changed it to Rita though. I'm not a Susan any more. I've called myself Rita – y' know, after Rita Mae Brown.

Frank (*blankly*)   Who?

Rita   Y' know, Rita Mae Brown – *Rubyfruit Jungle*. (*With serious reverence.*) Rita Mae Brown, she wrote *Rubyfruit Jungle*.

Frank   Ah.

Rita   Have you not read it? It's fantastic. D' y' want me to lend it to y'?

Frank   Erm, well, perhaps one day I might, erm . . .

But it's too late because she is already pulling her well-thumbed copy from her bag and showing it to him.

Rita   And that's who I named myself after. 'Cos I just love that book. Do you wanna lend it?

Frank Oh . . . um . . . well ah . . .

It's no good trying to avoid it. She presses it upon him.

Rita So what about you – what are you called?

Frank Frank.

Rita Oh, and were you named after someone?

Frank Well, not as far as I'm aware.

Rita Maybe your parents named you after the quality; y' know, 'Frank', 'frankness' – Eliot's brother –

Frank What?

Rita Y' know – Frank Ness. Eliot's brother. Eliot Ness.

Frank Oh! Eliot Ness. When you said Eliot I assumed you were referring to Tom – T.S. Eliot.

Rita T.S. Eliot? Have you read his stuff?

Frank Indeed I have, every last syllable.

Rita (*impressed*) Honest? I couldn't even get to the end of just one poem; I tried to read this thing called 'J. Arthur Prufrock' but I couldn't make any bleeding sense of it at all. I just gave up.

A beat.

I've not half got a lot to learn, haven't I?

Frank Did I hear you say you were a ladies' hairdresser?

Rita Yeh.

Frank Are you good at it?

Rita (*shrugging*) I am when I wanna be. Most of the time I don't wanna be, though. They get on my nerves.

Frank Who?

Rita The women, the customers. They never tell y' things that matter. Like, doin' a perm; well, y' can't use a strong perm lotion on a head if it's been bleached with certain sorts of, y' know, cheap bleach. Because it makes all the hair break off, y' see. But at least once a month I'll get a customer comin' in for a perm an' she'll swear blind that she's had no bleaching done; but I can tell! I can see it. But she swears to God; so y' go ahead an' do the perm and she comes out the drier with half an inch of stubble.

Frank   And are you able to do anything about that?

Rita   Yeh. Flog her a wig!

Frank   Good God!

Rita   The pensioners are the worst – they're dead vain, y' know – it doesn't matter how old they are; so they'll never crack on if they're wearin' somethin' like a hearin' aid. So y' get your scissors an' start trimmin' away, next thing is, snip! Another granny gone deaf for a fortnight.

Frank   You sound like something of a liability.

Rita   I am. But they expect too much. They walk into the hairdresser's and expect to walk out an hour later as a different person. I tell them, I'm just a hairdresser, not a plastic surgeon. See, most of them, that's why they come the hairdresser's – because they want to be changed. But if you wanna change y' have to do it from the inside, don't y'? Know like I'm doin' . . . tryin' to do. Do you think I will? Think I'll be able to do it.

Frank   Well, that really depends upon you, on how committed you are. Are you sure that you're absolutely serious about this?

Rita   I'm dead serious. Look, I know I take the piss an' that but I'm dead serious really. I am. I just take the piss because I'm not, y' know, confident. But I want to be. I want to know.

Frank   Everything!

She nods. He looks at her.

Rita   What y' lookin' at me like that for?

Frank   Because I think you're really rather marvellous.

Rita   For God's sake! Now who's taking the piss?

Frank   Don't you recognise a compliment?

Rita   Oh, sod off!

Frank   It's so long since I paid a compliment to anyone, I barely recognise it myself. (*He forces himself to change gear.*) So! Come on; what I want to know is why – what is it that's suddenly led you to doing this?

Rita   What, comin' here?

Frank   Yes.

Rita   Oh, it's not sudden. I've been realisin' for ages that I was . . . slightly out of step. I'm twenty-six. I should have had a baby by now; everyone expects it – I'm sure my husband thinks I'm infertile. He's always goin' on about havin' babies. We've been tryin' for two years now; but I'm still on the pill! See, I don't want a baby yet. I wanna find myself first, discover myself. Do you understand that?

He nods.

Yeh. They wouldn't round our way. I've tried to explain it to my husband but between you an' me I think he's just thick! No, not *thick*; blind, that's what he is. He can't see, because he doesn't *want* to see. If I try an' do anything different he gets a gob on him; even if I'm just reading or watchin' somethin' different on the telly he gets really narked. I just used to tell him to piss off but then I realised it was no good just doin' that an' what I should do is try an' explain to him. An' I tried; I tried explainin' to him how I wanted a better way of livin' my life. For once he listened. An' I even believed he understood because he said he felt the same as me – but all he meant was he was fed up livin' on our estate so we should start saving and try and move out to somewhere like Formby. Formby! Jesus, even if it was a new house I wanted I wouldn't move out to Formby. I hate that hole. Don't you?

Frank   Mm.

Rita   Whereabouts do you live?

Frank   Oh, erm, up towards Southport.

She realises and cringes.

Frank   Can I offer you another drink?

She shakes her head.

You don't mind if I do?

Rita   It's your brain cells.

Frank   All dead long ago, I'm afraid.

But now any mirth/playfulness has evaporated from him. He drinks with a kind of grimness that has only previously been hinted at.

Rita   When d' you actually, y' know, start teaching me?

Frank   What can I possibly teach you?

Rita   Everythin'

Frank   Everything.

A beat.

I'll make a bargain with you, yes? I'll teach you everything I know . . . but if I do that then you must promise never to come back here . . . because there's nothing here for you! You see I never . . . I didn't want to teach this course in the first place; allowed myself to be talked into it. But I knew it was wrong and seeing you only confirms my suspicion. My dear, it's not your fault, just the luck of the draw that you got assigned to me; but get me you did. And the thing is, between you, me and the walls, I'm really rather an appalling teacher. Most of the time that doesn't really matter – appalling teaching is quite in order when most of my students are themselves fairly appalling. And the others manage to get by despite me. But you, young woman, you are quite, quite different, you are seeking a very great deal indeed; and I'm afraid I cannot provide it. Everything I know – and you must listen to this – is that I know absolutely nothing. (*Beat.*) Added to which I don't like the hours of this Open University malarkey, intolerably bloody unsocial – when the sun's gone over the yardarm, my dear, I really should be in the pub! I can be really a rather good teacher when I'm in the pub. Four pints of weak Guinness and I can be as witty as Wilde, as pithy as Swift, as illuminating as . . . well! I'm sorry. There are other tutors – I'll make all the necessary arrangements and no doubt the college will be in touch.

Rita *slowly turns, collects her things and goes to the door. She goes out, closing the door behind her. Suddenly though, the inner door handle is being furiously turned as* **Rita** *tries to get back in. However, it being that door it won't open again. We hear frantic and repeated knocking.*

Rita (*off*)   Let me in . . . open this door . . . let me back in . . . open the door.

Frank (*calling*)   Go away!

Rita (*off*)   Wait a minute . . . open this door . . . listen . . .

Frank   Leave me alone. There are other tutors, I've told you I –

Rita (*off*)   You're my tutor! I don't want another tutor . . .

Frank   For God's sake, woman! I've told you . . .

Rita (*off*)   You are my tutor!

Frank   I've told you, I don't *want* to teach you. Why come to me?

And the door finally gives. **Rita** *enters.*

Rita   Because you're a crazy mad piss artist who wants to throw his students through the window. An' I *like* you. Don't you recognise a compliment? And when I come back next week I'm gonna bring my scissors an' give you a haircut.

Frank   You are not coming back next week.

Rita   I am! An' you're gettin' your hair cut.

Frank   Oh, I don't think so.

Rita   I suppose you wanna walk 'round like that, do y'?

Frank   Like what?

Rita (*turning back just before she exits*)   Like a geriatric hippy!

Rita *exits.*

Blackout.

Scene Two

The desk light is on.

Frank *is standing by the window, looking out. He glances at his watch and then peers out of the window again. He goes across to the bookcase, removes a few volumes and stares in at the bottle of scotch. For a moment he is tempted. But he resists and replaces the books. Walking away from the bookcase he goes to the window and looks out again. He glances at his watch once more. And then, changing his mind again:*

Frank   Oh, sod it!

*He heads for the bookcase, pulling out books as he looks for the bottle. Only, as he does so he becomes aware of a noise. He turns and realises that the door handle is being turned. Quickly replacing the books he moves towards the door, hesitating and then suddenly pulling it open to reveal **Rita**, oil can in hand.*

Rita   I was just oilin' it for y'. Well, I knew you'd never get around to it. (*Handing him the can as she brushes past him and enters the room.*) Y' can have that.

Frank   Oh! (*Dubiously.*) Thank you.

He watches as she wanders around the room.

Rita   What y' lookin' at?

Frank   Do you never just walk into a room and sit down?

Rita   No. Not when it's a room like this. I love it.

A beat.

How d' y' make a room like this?

Frank   I don't *do* anything.

Rita   Ah! That's the secret.

Frank   There is no secret. I just moved in. And the rest just sort of . . . happened.

Rita   Yeh, that's 'cos you've got taste.

A beat.

I'm gonna have a room like this one day; there's nothin' phoney about it; everything's in its right place. It's like wherever you've put something down . . . it's grown to fit there.

Frank   You mean it's a mess!

Rita   Well, yeh. But . . . but it's like . . . it's like it's a lovely mess.

Frank   Well . . . I suppose that over the years it might have acquired a certain patina.

Rita   Yeh. That's what I meant. That sounds like a line from a romantic film, doesn't it? 'Over the years your face has acquired a certain patina.'

A beat.

You haven't been drinkin', have y'?

Frank   Erm . . . well, since you ask, no . . . as a matter of fact.

Rita Is that because of me? Because of what I said to y' last week?

Frank What? You think where so many others have failed, you have reformed me!

Rita (*moving to the window*)   I don't wanna reform y'. You can do what you like. (*Deliberately changing gear.*) I love that lawn. It looks the way I always imagined somewhere like Eton or Harrow or one of those public schools to look. When I was a kid I always wanted to go to a boarding school.

Frank God forbid! Whatever for?

Rita I always thought they sounded great, schools like that. Y' know with a tuck shop and a matron and jolly hockey sticks; and there was always a pair of kids called Jones Major an' Jones Minor. I always loved that.

Frank What sort of a school *did* you go to?

Rita Just normal; like all the other schools by us; borin', ripped-up books, glass everywhere, knives and fights an' sadists – an' that was just the staff room. No, they tried their best, I suppose, always tellin' us we stood much more of a chance if we studied and worked hard. But studyin' was just for the geeks an' the wimps, wasn't it? See, if I'd started takin' school seriously then I would have had to become different from my mates; an' that's not allowed.

Frank Not allowed by whom?

Rita By y' mates, y' family, by everyone. So y' never admit that school could be anythin' other than useless an' irrelevant. An' what you've really got to be into are things like music an' clothes and gettin' pissed an' coppin' off an' all that kind of stuff. Not that I didn't go along with it because I did. But at the same time, there was always somethin' tappin' away in my head, tryin' to tell me I might have got it all wrong. But I'd just put the music back on or buy another dress an' stop worryin'. 'Cos there's always something that can make y' forget. An' so y' keep on goin', tellin' y'self that life is great – there's always another club to go to, a new feller to be chasin', a laugh an' a joke with the girls. Till one day, you just stop an' own up to yourself. Y' say, 'Is this it? Is this the absolute maximum that I can expect from this livin' lark?' An' that's the really big moment that is. Because that is when you've got to decide whether it's gonna be another change of dress or a change in yourself. And it's really tempting to go out an' get that other dress. Because that way it's easy; y' know that you won't be upsettin' anyone or hurtin' anyone – apart from y'self! An' sometimes it's easier to do that, to take the pain y'self instead of hurtin' those around y'; those who don't want you to change.

Frank   But . . . you . . . did it . . . You managed to resist another new dress.

Rita   You mean y' can't tell? Would y' look at the state of this? I haven't bought myself a new dress for the past twelve months. An' I'm not gonna get one either; not till I pass my first exam. An' then I'll get a proper dress, the sort of dress you'd only see on a educated woman, on the sort of woman who knows the difference between Jane Austin and . . . erm . . . and Ethel Austen!

A beat.

OK. Can we start?

Frank   Good idea. Yes, yes. (*He locates a couple of sheets of A4 paper on his desk.*) All right; now look, this piece you wrote for me on, what was it called . . . ?

Rita   *Rubyfruit Jungle* by Rita Mae Brown.

Frank   Yes, well, the thing is, erm, it was, how can I say it . . .

Rita   Shite?

Frank   No no . . . the thing is, it was an appreciation and erm, a reasonably structured outline of the plot. But you've made no attempt to explore whatever themes there are or how character is portrayed and developed or what kind of narrative is being employed. In short, you haven't really brought any criticism to bear.

Rita   But I don't *want* to criticise *Rubyfruit Jungle*! Because I think it's brilliant!

Frank   No no, I'm not talking about criticising, being critical in a censorious way; I'm talking about analytical criticism.

Rita   What's the difference?

Frank   Well, as far as possible you should approach criticism as being purely objective. You see, you might consider . . . erm . . . what's it called . . .

Rita   *Rubyfruit Jungle.*

Frank   Yes, now you might consider . . . *Rubyfruit Jungle* . . .

Rita   By Rita Mae Brown.

Frank   . . . by Rita Mae Brown . . . to be, what did you say, brilliant! But Rita, that is *not* criticism; it is mere opinion. You see, it's subjective. And in criticism there is no place for the subjective, for the sentimental, for the partial or partisan. Literary criticism should be detached and thoroughly supported by reference to established literary critique. Now bearing all of that in mind I'd like you to give me a considered response to your reading of *Howards End*.

Rita   What, now?

Frank   Yes. You have read it?

Rita   Yeh! I've read it.

Frank   So? (*Prompting.*) *Howards End*?

Rita (*adopting suitable posture*)   *Howards End* by Mr E.M. Forster is one really crap book!

Frank   What!

Rita   In fact it's even crappier than crap!

Frank   Oh really? And who the hell are you citing in support of that particular thesis, F.R. Leavis?

Rita   No! Me!

Frank   What have I just said? Me is subjective!

Rita   Well, it's what I think!

Frank   You think one of the most considered novels of the twentieth century is, 'crap'! Well, perhaps you'll do me the courtesy of explaining why you think it's, quote, 'crap', unquote.

Rita   Yeh, all right, yeh! I will tell y'! It's crap because the feller who wrote it was a louse. Because halfway through that book I could hardly go on readin' because he, Mr bleedin' E.M. Forster says, quote – 'we are not concerned with the poor' – unquote! That's why it's crap. That's why I could barely keep on readin' it, that's why!

Frank (*astounded*)   Because he said, 'we are not concerned with the poor'?

Rita   Yeh! That's right!

Frank   But he wasn't writing about the poor.

Rita   When he wrote that book the conditions of the poor in this country were appalling an' he's sayin' he couldn't care less, Mr E.M. soddin' Foster.

Frank   Forster!

Rita   I don't really care what he was called – sittin' up there in his ivory tower an' sayin' he couldn't care less.

Frank *begins to laugh.*

Rita   Don't laugh at me!

Frank But this is madness! You cannot interpret E.M.
Forster from a Marxist perspective.

Rita Why not?

Frank Look, before discussing any of this I said no
subjectivity, no sentimentality.

Rita I wasn't being sentimental.

Frank Of course you were! You wanted Forster to
concern himself with the poor. Literature can ignore the
poor.

Rita Well, I think that's immoral.

Frank Amoral! (*Beat.*) Have you any idea what kind of a
mark you'd get if you approached Forster in this way during
an examination?

Rita No! An' I don't care!

Frank Well, in that case we're going to have to make you
care, aren't we? Because if I'm going to teach you and
you're going to learn then I'm afraid you'll . . .

Rita All right! All right! But I hated that book. Can't we
do somethin' else? Can't we do a book that I like?

Frank But books you *like* and books that will form the
basis of your examination are extremely unlikely to be one
and the same. The examiners, God help them, may never
have heard of . . . *Rubyfruit Jungle* . . . or Rita Mae Brown.
And that is why you are going to have to learn how to
discipline that mind of yours, learn how to focus and
concentrate and . . .

Rita Are you married?

Frank Oh, for God's sake!

Rita Are y' though? What's y' wife called?

Frank Is my wife of the remotest relevance here?

Rita Well, you should know that – you married her.

Frank   All right! No, she's not relevant. We parted a long long time ago. OK?

Rita   I'm sorry.

Frank   Sorry for what?

Rita   For asking. For bein' nosey.

Frank   OK. But look, the thing about Forster and a book like *Howards End* is that . . .

Rita   Why did you split up?

Frank (*after a beat*)   Perhaps you'd like to take notes, mm? Then when you have to answer a question on Forster, you can treat the examiners to a dissertation on Frank's marriage!

Rita   Oh, go 'way! It's only 'cos I'm interested.

Frank (*after a beat*)   We split up, Rita, because of poetry.

Rita   Go 'way.

Frank   One day . . . my then wife pointed out to me that for the preceding fifteen years my output as a poet had dealt exclusively with that brief period in which we had . . . *discovered* each other.

Rita   Are you a poet?

Frank   Was – an extremely minor one – and so, to give me something fresh to fire the muse, she left me. A very selfless and noble woman, my ex-wife – she sacrificed her marriage for the sake of literature.

Rita   An' what happened?

Frank   Oh, it did the trick. My loss was literature's great gain.

Rita   You started writing a whole load of good new stuff?

Frank   No, I stopped writing altogether.

Rita (*after a beat*)   Are you takin' the piss?

Frank   No.

Rita   People don't split up because of things like that, because of poetry an' literature . . .

Frank   No?

Rita   Did you never write any famous poems?

Frank (*laughing*)   No. I published a couple of small collections. Sold a few here and there.

Rita   Can y' still get them? I'll buy one of your books.

Frank   I'm afraid they're all long out of print. And anyway I don't think it's the kind of stuff that you would have enjoyed.

Rita   Why?

Frank   Because, Rita, it's the sort of poetry that you *can't* understand! Unless, that is, you happen to have a detailed knowledge of literary allusion.

Rita   So d'you live on your own now?

Frank   No! I live with someone; an ex-student, she's now a tutor here. She's very caring, very tolerant, admires me enormously and spends a good deal of time with her head in the oven.

Rita   Tryin' to kill herself.

Frank   No, she just likes to watch the ratatouille cook or, as Julia's recently renamed it, 'the stopout's stew'.

Rita   Is that you? Who stops out?

Frank   Occasionally.

Rita   For how long?

Frank (*slightly coy*)   Two . . . three days . . . only now and then . . .

Rita   Why?

Frank   Now come on, look, that's enough of that; let's . . .

Rita   If you were mine an' y' stopped out for days, y' wouldn't get back in!

Frank   Ah, but Rita, if I was yours would I even consider stopping out for days?

Rita   Don't you like her, Julia?

Frank   I like her enormously. It's myself that I'm not too fond of.

Rita   But you're great.

Frank   A vote of confidence – thank you. Only, I'm afraid, Rita, that eventually you'll find there's less to me than meets the eye.

Rita   See – you can say dead clever things like that. I wish I could just talk like that, it's brilliant.

Frank   Yes, all right. Now, come on, *Howards End* . . .

Rita   Oh hey! Leave that. I like just talkin' to y', it's great. That's what they do wrong in schools – they get y' goin' and then y' all havin' a great time talkin' about somethin' that's dead interestin' but the next thing is they wanna turn it into a lesson. Like we was out with this teacher once, y' know outside school on some project an' I'm right at the back with these other kids an' we saw this fantastic-lookin' bird; it was all plumed an' coloured and dead out of place around our way. So I was just about to shout out an' tell Miss about it but this kid next to me said, 'Keep y' mouth shut or she'll make us write a bleedin' essay on it!'

Frank (*ruefully*)   Yes! It's what we do, Rita; we pluck birds from the sky and nail them down to learn how they fly.

Rita   You'd think there was something wrong with education to hear you talk.

Frank   Yes and perhaps there is.

Rita   So why are y' givin' me an education?

Frank   Because it's what *you* wanted. If it was up to me, what I'd like to do is take you by the hand and run out of this room for ever.

Rita   Oh, be serious!

Frank   I am, Rita. I am! Right now there are a thousand things I'd rather do than teach – most of them with you, young woman.

Rita   Oh, go 'way! You just like sayin' things like that!

Frank   Do I?

Rita   Y' know y' do.

Frank   Oh Rita! Why didn't you walk in here twenty years ago?

Frank   Because I don't think they would have accepted me at the age of six.

Frank   You know what I mean.

Rita   I know. But it's not twenty years ago, Frank. It's now – you're there an' I'm here.

Frank   Yes and you're here for an education. Now come on! Forster.

Rita   Oh, forget him!

Frank   Now you listen to me! You want to learn, you want me to teach you. Well, that, I'm afraid, means a lot of work, for you as well as me. You've barely had a basic schooling, you've never even sat a formal examination let alone passed one. Possessing a hungry mind is not in itself a guarantee of any kind of success.

Rita   All right, but I just don't like *Howards* bleedin' *End*.

Frank (*suddenly sharp*)   Then go back to what you do like and stop wasting my time. You go off and buy yourself a new dress and I'll go to the pub!

A beat.

Rita   Is that you puttin' your foot down?

Frank   Yes!

Rita   Y' dead impressive when you're angry.

Frank   Forster!

Rita (*picking up pen and essay papers*)   All right, all right –
Forster, Forster fuckin' Forster; 'Does the repeated use of
the phrase "only connect" suggest that in reality E.M.
Forster was a frustrated electrician?'

Blackout.

Scene Three

Frank *is working at his desk, absorbed in re-reading* **Rita***'s essay as*
Rita *herself rushes in, slightly out of breath, hurriedly removing her
coat and quickly trying to get herself organised.*

Rita   Am I late? I'm sorry I'm late . . . I bleedin' hate it
when that happens; I thought I'd easily be out of the shop
by five tonight. I didn't have anyone booked in after four
o'clock so I thought I'd easy get away by five, no worry. But
bloody half past four one of my regulars showed up; could I
do her a quick wash an' blow dry because she'd met this
feller who's got a Chinese chippie in Childwall. *He's* not
Chinese so it's not really a Chinese chippie – it's sort of . . .
must be fusion, I suppose. Well, he phoned her up out of the
blue this afternoon 'cos he's just copped a couple of tickets
for an exhibition of state-of-the-art refrigeration units an'
walk-in freezers. She said she doesn't even fancy him really.
But she's always wanted a walk-in freezer herself . . .

Rita *finally becomes aware of* **Frank***, staring at her as if she's
something from another planet.*

Rita   Oh God, I'm sorry, sorry; it's bein' in that shop
every day – I think it must be catching; that's what I have to

listen to, all day every day. Anyway, I'm sorry I'm late. I hate bein' late when I'm comin' here.

Frank   Let's forget about that. I want to talk about this that you sent me.

Rita (*knowing*)   Oh, that!

Frank   Yes! In response to the question, 'Suggest how you might resolve the staging difficulties inherent in a production of Ibsen's *Peer Gynt*', you have written, quote, 'Do it on the radio', unquote.

Rita   Precisely!

Frank   Precisely what?

Rita   Precisely do it on the radio.

Frank   And that is the entire essay?

Rita (*squirming*)   Well . . . we were . . . we were just dead busy in the shop this week.

Frank   You write your essays at work.

She nods.

Frank   Why?

Rita   Denny gets really pissed off if I work at home. He doesn't like me doin' this course. I can't be bothered arguin' with him.

Frank   But you can't produce work that's as thin as this.

Rita   Is it wrong?

Frank   It's not a question of whether it's *wrong*. It's the fact of . . .

Rita   See, I know it's on the short side . . . but, but I thought it was the right answer.

Frank   Well, it's the basis for an argument, Rita, but *one line* is hardly an essay.

Rita   I know but I just didn't have much time this week so I sort . . . sort of . . . *encapsulated* all my ideas in one line.

Frank   But it's not good enough.

Rita   Why not?

Frank   It just isn't.

Rita   But that's bleedin' stupid because you say, don't y', that . . . one line . . . of exquisite poetry says . . . infinitely more than a thousand pages of second-rate prose.

Frank   Yes. But you're not writing poetry! You are supposed to be writing an essay and what I'm trying to make you understand is that whoever was marking this would want more than 'do it on the radio'! (*Changing gear.*) Look, there's a way of answering examination questions that is . . . expected. It's a sort of accepted ritual. It's a game, with rules. And you have to observe those rules. Poets can ignore those rules; poets can break every rule in the book; poets are not trying to pass examinations. But Rita, you are. And therefore you must observe the rules. When I was at university there was a student taking his final theology examination. He sat down in the hall, opened the exam paper, took out his pen and wrote, 'God knows all the answers.' Whereupon he handed in his paper, and left.

Rita (*impressed*)   Did he?

Frank   Yes, he did. And when it was time to collect his results he received a piece of paper on which were the words, 'And God also gives out the marks!'

Rita   Did he fail?

Frank   Of *course* he failed! And rightly in my view because a clever answer is not necessarily the best answer.

Rita   I wasn't trying to be clever; I was just run off me feet all this week so I never had time . . .

Frank   All right, yes, yes, I know. But you have got some time now. And I want you to give it just a quarter of an hour or so adding some considered argument to this. 'In attempting to resolve the staging difficulties in *Peer Gynt* I would present it on the radio because . . .' and then outline your reasons, supporting them wherever possible with quotes from accepted authorities. (*He switches the desk light on.*) All right?

Rita   Yeh. All right.

Rita *picks up her things and, helped by* **Frank**, *moves across to the second desk/table.*

Frank   Now you're sure you understand?

Rita   D'you think I'm thick?

As **Rita** *settles herself at her desk,* **Frank** *returns to his own desk and busies himself reading and marking an essay.* **Rita** *finally gets down to work. But after a few moments she stops, deep in thought.*

Rita   Y'know Peer Gynt? He was searchin' for the meaning of life, wasn't he?

Frank   Put at its briefest, yes.

Rita   Yeh.

Beat.

I was doin' this woman's hair on Wednesday . . .

Frank   Rita!

Rita   I'm gonna do this, don't worry, I'll do it! But I just wanna tell y'; I was doin' her hair an' I was dead bored with what the others were talkin' about in the shop so I said to my customer, 'Do you know about Peer Gynt?' She just thought it was a new kind of conditioner! So I told her all about it, the play? An' y' know somethin', she was dead interested.

Frank (*uninterested*)   Was she?

Rita   She said to me, this woman, after I'd told her all about it, she said: 'I wish I could go off searchin' for the

meanin' of life.' There's loads of them round by us who feel
like that. Because there is no meaning!

A beat as **Rita** *ponders for a moment and* **Frank** *remains absorbed
in his work.*

Rita   Frank, y' know culture, know the word 'culture',
well, it doesn't just mean goin' to the opera an' the ballet
and all that, does it?

Frank   No.

Rita   It means a way of livin', doesn't it? (*She pauses.*) Well,
we've got no culture.

Frank   Who hasn't?

Rita   Me; an' the people I come from – people I work
with, live with, grew up with – us, we've got no culture.

Frank   Of course you have.

Rita   What? D' y' mean like that 'working-class culture'
thing?

Frank   Well . . . yes.

Rita   Yeh. I've read about that. I've never seen it though.

Frank   Then look around you.

Rita   I do. But I don't see any culture; I just see everyone
pissed or stoned tryin' to find their way from one empty day
to the next. There's more culture in a pot of yoghurt. Y'
daren't say somethin' like that round our way though,
because they're proud; an' they'll tell you we have got
culture, doin' the pub quiz, goin' the club, singin' karaoke.

Frank   But if they're content with that, if that's what
people want then surely they've got the . . .

Rita   But they *don't* want that! There is no contentment.
Because there's no meanin' left. (*Beat.*) Sometimes, when y'
hear the old ones tellin' stories about the past, y' know,
about the war or when they were all strugglin', fightin' for

food and clothes and houses, their eyes light up while
they're tellin y' because there was some meanin'*then. But
what's . . . what's stupid is that *now* . . . now that most of
them have got some kind of a house an' there is food an'
money around, they're better off but, honest, they know
they've got nothin' as well – because the meanin's all gone;
so there's nothin' to believe in. It's like there's this sort of
disease but no one mentions it; everyone behaves as though
it's normal, y' know, inevitable, that there's vandalism an'
violence an' houses burnt out and wrecked by the people
they were built for. But this disease, it just keeps on bein'
hidden; because everyone's caught up in the 'Got-to-Have'
game, all runnin' round like headless chickens chasin' the
latest got-to-have tellies an' got-to-have cars, got-to-have
haircuts an' got-to-have phones an' all the other got-to-have
garbage that leaves y' wonderin' why you've still got nothin'
– even when you've got it. (*Beat.*) I suppose it's just like me,
isn't it, y' know when I was buyin' dresses, keepin' the
disease covered up all the time.

Frank (*after a beat*)   Did you never consider taking a course
in politics?

Rita   Politics? Go 'way, I hate politics. I'm just tellin' y'
about round our way. I wanna be on *this* course. You know
what I learn from you about art an' literature, it feeds me,
inside. I can get through the rest of the week if I know I've
got comin' here to look forward to. (*Beat.*) Denny tried to
stop me comin' tonight. He tried to get me to go the pub
with him an' his mates. He hates me comin' here. It's like
druggies, isn't it? Addicts hate it when one of them tries to
break away. It makes me stronger comin' here. That's what
Denny's frightened of.

Frank   'Only connect'!

Rita   Oh, not faggie friggin' Forster again!

Frank   'Only connect' – you see what you've been doing?

Rita   Just tellin' y' about home.

Frank   Yes, and connecting: your dresses/society at large/consumerism; drugs and addiction/you and your husband – connecting.

Rita   Oh.

Frank   You see?

Rita   An' . . . an' in that book . . . no one does connect.

Frank   Yes! Irony.

Rita   Is that it? Is that all it means?

Frank   Not *all* of it but yes, that's the hub of it.

Rita   Why didn't you just explain that to me right from the start?

Frank   I could have done; but you'll have a much better understanding of something if you discover it in your own terms.

Rita   Aren't you clever?

Frank   Brilliant. Now! *Peer Gynt*.

Rita *returns to her desk and begins her work.* **Frank** *returns to his marking. We watch them, each absorbed in his/her work until* **Rita** *finishes writing and crosses to* **Frank***'s desk.*

Frank (*eventually looking up*)   What?

Rita   I've done it.

Frank   You've done it?

Rita *hands him the essay, from which he reads.*

'In attempting to resolve the staging difficulties in a production of Ibsen's *Peer Gynt*, I would present it as a radio play because, as Ibsen himself said, he wrote the play as a play for voices, never intending it to go on in a theatre. So if they had the radio in his day that's where he would have done it.'

He looks up at **Rita** *who is beaming with unabashed pride and delight.*

Blackout.

Scene Four

There is an 'atmosphere'. **Rita**, *still wearing outdoor coat/jacket, is standing, gazing out of the window, her back to* **Frank**.

Frank   What's wrong? You know this is getting to be a bit wearisome. When you come to this room you'll do anything except start work immediately. Couldn't you just come in prepared to work?

Pause.

Where's your essay?

Rita   I haven't got it.

Frank   You haven't done it.

Rita   I said I haven't *got* it.

Frank   You've lost it?

Rita   No.

Frank   Don't tell me! Last night, whilst you were asleep a couple of errant Oxbridge dons broke into your premises and appropriated your essay for their own highly dubious ends.

No reaction.

(*Gently.*) Rita!

She turns to face him.

Rita   It's burnt.

Frank   Burnt?

Rita So are all the Chekhov books you lent me. Denny found out I was still on the pill; it was my own fault, I'd left me prescription out. He burnt all me books.

Frank Oh Christ!

Rita I'm sorry. I'll buy y' some more.

Frank I wasn't referring to the books. Sod the books.

Rita Why can't he just let me get on with my learnin'? You'd think I was havin' a fuckin' affair the way he behaves.

Frank And aren't you?

Rita No! What time have I got for an affair? I'm busy enough findin' myself, let alone findin' someone else. I don't want anyone else. I've begun to find me – an' it's great, y' know, it is, Frank. It might sound selfish but all I want for the time bein' is what I'm findin' inside me. I certainly don't wanna be rushin' off with some feller, 'cos the first thing I'll have to do is forget about myself for the sake of him.

Frank Perhaps . . . perhaps your husband thinks you're having an affair with me.

Rita Oh, go 'way. You're just me teacher. I've told him.

Frank You've told him about me? What?

Rita I've – tch – I've tried to explain to him how you give me room to breathe. You just, like feed me without expectin' anythin' in return.

Frank (*after a beat*) And what did he say to that?

Rita He didn't. I was out for a while. When I came back he'd burnt me books an' papers, most of them. I said to him, y' soft get, even if I was havin' an affair there's no point burnin' me books, is there. I'm not havin' it off with Anton Chekhov! He said, 'I wouldn't put it past you to shack up with a foreigner.'

Frank What are you going to do?

Rita   I'll order some new copies for y' an' I'll do the essay again.

Frank   I mean about your husband.

Rita   I've told him, I said, 'There's no point cryin' over spilt milk, most of the books are gone, but if you touch my *Peer Gynt* I'll kill y''.'

Frank   Tch. Be serious.

Rita   I was!

Frank   Do you love him?

Rita   I see him lookin' at me sometimes, an' I know what he's thinkin'; he's wonderin' where the girl he married has gone to. He even brings me presents sometimes, hopin' that the presents'll make her come back. But she can't, because she's gone, an' I've taken her place.

Frank   Do you want to abandon this course?

Rita   No. No!

Frank   When art and literature begin to take the place of life itself, perhaps it's time to . . .

Rita   But it's *not* takin' the place of life, it's *providin'* me with life. He wants to take life away from me; he wants me to stop rockin' the coffin, that's all. Comin' here, doin' this, it's given me more life than I've had in years, an' he should be able to see that. Well, if he doesn't see that, if he doesn't want me when I'm alive, then I'm certainly not just gonna lie down an' die for him. I told him I'd only have a baby when I had a choice. But he doesn't understand. He thinks we've got choice because we can go into a pub that sells eight different kinds of lager. He thinks we've got choice already: choice between Everton an' Liverpool, choosin' which washin' powder, choosin' between one shitty school an' the next, between jobs for jokers or stayin' on the dole. He thinks we've *got* choice already because there's thirty-eight satellite channels to watch.

Frank   Yes. Well, perhaps your husband –

Rita   No! I don't come here to talk about him. Why was Chekhov a comic genius?

Frank   Rita! Don't you think that for tonight we could give the class a miss?

Rita   No, I want to know. I've got to do this. He can burn me books an' me papers but if it's all in my head then he can't touch it. It's like that with you, isn't it? You've got it all inside.

Frank   Let's leave it for tonight. Let's go to the pub and drink pots of Guinness and talk.

Rita   I've got to do this, Frank. I've got to. I want to talk about Chekhov.

Frank   You don't think you should be talking about you and your husband?

Rita   I don't want to.

Frank (*recognising the determination*)   All right, OK . . . (*He goes to the bookcase and lifts down books.*) Chekhov. C for Chekhov. We'll talk about Chekhov and pretend this is the pub.

Rita (*seeing the bottles*)   Why d' y' keep it stashed behind there?

Frank   A little arrangement I have with my immediate employers. It's called 'discretion'. They didn't tell me to stop drinking, they told me to stop displaying the signs.

Rita   Do you actually *like* drinking?

Frank   I adore it. You see, Rita, the great thing about the booze is that one is never bored when drinking. Or boring for that matter; the booze has this marvellous capacity for making one believe that underneath all the talk one is actually *saying* something.

Rita (*after a beat*)   Know when you were a poet, Frank, did you drink then?

Frank   Some. Not as much as now.

Rita   Why did you stop being a poet?

Frank   That is a pub question.

Rita   Well. I thought we were pretendin' this was the pub.

Frank   In which we would discuss Chekhov!

Rita   Well, he's second on the bill. You're on first. Go on, why did you stop?

Frank (*sighing*)   I didn't stop, Rita, so much as realise I never was. I'd simply got it wrong. Instead of creating poetry I spent – oh – years trying to create literature.

Rita   But . . . but I thought that's what poets did.

Frank   What?

Rita   Y' know, create literature.

Frank   No no no; poets should confine themselves to creating poetry; poets should do their damnedest not to believe in literature.

Rita   I don't understand that.

Frank   You will, Rita; one day you will.

Rita   Huh. Sometimes I wonder if I'll ever understand any of it. It's like startin' all over again, y' know with a different language. Like I read that Chekhov play an' I thought it was dead sad, it was tragic; people committin' suicide an' the Constantin kid's tryin' to produce his masterpiece while they're all laughin' at him? It is, it's tragic. But then I read the blurb about it an' everyone's goin' on about Chekhov bein' 'this comic genius'.

Frank   Yes, but they don't mean comedy like – erm – well, it's not jokes, gags; it's not . . . stand-up comedy. Have you ever seen Chekhov in the theatre?

Rita No. Does he go?

Frank Have you ever been to the theatre?

Rita No.

Frank You should, you should go.

Rita Hey! Why don't we go tonight?

Frank Me go to the theatre? God, no, I detest the theatre.

Rita Well, why the hell are y' sendin' me?

Frank Because *you* want to know.

Rita Well, you come with me.

Frank Oh, certainly! And how would I explain that to Julia?

Rita Just tell her y' comin' to the theatre with me.

Frank 'Julia, I shall not be in for dinner tonight as I am going to the theatre with ravishing Rita.'

Rita Oh, sod off.

Frank I'm being quite serious.

Rita Would she really be jealous?

Frank If she knew I was at the theatre with an irresistible thing like you? Rita, it would be deaf-and-dumb breakfasts for a week.

Rita Why?

Frank Why not?

Rita I dunno – I just thought . . .

Frank Rita, as ludicrous as it may seem to you, even a woman who possesses an MA is not above common jealousy.

Rita   Well, what's she got to be jealous of me for? I'm not gonna try an' rape y' in the middle of *The Seagull*.

Frank   What a terrible pity. You just might have made theatre exciting for me again.

Rita   Come on, Frank. Come with me. Y' never tell the truth you, do y'?

Frank   What do y' mean?

Rita   You always . . . *evade* it, don't y', with jokes an' that. Come on, come to the theatre with me. We'll have a laugh . . .

Frank   Will we?

Rita   Yeh. C'mon, wc'll ring Julia. (*She picks up* **Frank***'s phone.*)

Frank   What?

Rita   C'mon, what's your number?

Frank (*taking the receiver from her and replacing it*)   We will *not* ring Julia. Anyway, Julia's out tonight.

Rita   So what will you do, spend the entire night in the pub?

Frank   Yes.

Rita   Come with me, Frank, y'll have a better time than y'will in the pub.

Frank   Will I?

Rita   Course y'will.

Frank (*considering*)   What is it you want to see?

Rita   *The Importance of Bein'* ... what's-his-name.

Frank   *The Importance*? It's not on at the moment.

Rita   It is – I passed the church hall on the bus an' there was a poster . . .

Frank   An *amateur* production?

Rita   What?

Frank   Are you suggesting I miss a night in the pub to watch *The Importance of Being Earnest* played by a bunch of bloody amateurs in a church hall?

Rita   It doesn't matter who's doin' it! It's the same play, isn't it?

Frank   Well! I wouldn't be so sure of that, Rita . . .

Rita   Oh, come on – hurry up – I'm dead excited. I've never seen a live play before.

During the following they prepare to leave the room – collecting bags, coats, switching off lamps.

Frank   And there's no guarantee you'll see a 'live' play tonight.

Rita   Why? Just 'cos they're amateurs? Y've got to give them a chance, Frank. They have to learn somewhere. An' anyway, they might be good.

Frank   Yes . . .

Rita   Oh, you're an awful snob, aren't y'?

Frank   Am I? All right then – come on. (*He switches off the desk lamp.*)

Rita   Have you seen it before?

Frank   Of course I have. (*He switches off the standard lamp.*)

Rita   Well, don't you go tellin' me what happens, will y'? Don't go spoilin' it for me.

They exit.

Blackout.

Scene Five

It is lunchtime as **Frank** *enters.*

He puts down his things, switches on the radio (Radio Four) from which we hear the weather forecast directly preceding The World At One. **Frank** *takes out his lunch and sits at his desk eating and reading a book, the cover of which we recognise as being* Rubyfruit Jungle.

Rita *suddenly bursts into the room, out of breath from running.*

Frank *switches off the radio.*

Frank   What are you doing here? It's Thursday, you . . .

Rita   I know I shouldn't be here, it's me dinner hour, but listen, I've got to tell someone, have y' got a few minutes, can y' spare –

Frank   My God, what is it?

Rita   I had to come an' tell y', Frank, last night, I went to the theatre! A proper one, a professional theatre.

Frank   For God's sake, you had me worried, I thought it was something serious.

Rita   It was, it was Shakespeare, I thought it was gonna be dead borin' but it wasn't – it was brilliant. I'm gonna do an essay on it.

Frank   Come on, which one was it?

Rita
'. . . Out, out, brief candle!
Life's but a walking shadow, a poor player
That struts and frets his hour upon the stage
And then is heard no more. It is a tale
Told by an idiot, full of sound and fury.
Signifying nothing.'

Frank   Ah, *Romeo and Juliet.*

Rita   Tch. Frank! Be serious. I learnt that today from the book. Look, I went out an' bought the book. Isn't it great? What I couldn't get over is how excitin' it was. Wasn't his wife a cow, eh? An' that fantastic bit where he meets Macduff an' he thinks he's all invincible. I was on the edge of me seat at that bit. I wanted to shout out an' tell Macbeth, warn him.

Frank   You didn't, did you?

Rita   Nah. Y' can't do that in a theatre, can y'? It was brilliant though. It was like a thriller.

Frank   Well, you'll have to go and see more Shakespeare.

Rita   I'm goin' to. *Macbeth*'s a tragedy, isn't it?

Frank   Yes, it is.

Rita   Right.

Beat.

Well, I just – I just had to tell someone who'd understand.

Frank   I'm honoured that you chose me.

Rita   I better get back. I've left a customer in the shop. If I don't get a move on there'll be another tragedy.

Frank   No. There won't be a tragedy.

Rita   There will, y' know. I know this woman, she's dead fussy. If her lo' lights don't come out right there'll be blood an' guts everywhere.

Frank   Which might be quite tragic – but it won't be a tragedy.

Rita   What?

Frank   Well – erm – look; the tragedy of the drama has nothing to do with the sort of tragic event you're talking about. Macbeth is flawed by his ambition – yes?

Rita   Yeh. Go on.

Frank   Erm – it's that flaw which forces him to take the inevitable steps towards his own doom. You see? Whereas, Rita, a woman's hair being ruined, or – or the sort of thing you read in the paper that's reported as being tragic, 'Man Killed by Falling Tree', that is *not* a tragedy.

Rita   It is for the poor sod under the tree.

Frank   Yes, it's tragic, absolutely tragic. But it's not a *tragedy* in the way that *Macbeth* is a tragedy. You see, in dramatic terms, tragedy is something that is absolutely inevitable, preordained almost. Now, look, even without ever having even heard the story of *Macbeth* you wanted to shout out, to warn him and prevent him going on, didn't you? But you wouldn't have been able to stop him, would you?

Rita   No.

Frank   And why is that?

Rita   'Cos they would have thrown me out of the theatre.

Frank   No no no no, what I mean is that your warning would have been ignored. He's warned in the play, constantly warned. But he can't go back. He still treads the path to doom. But, you see, the poor old fellow under the tree hasn't arrived there by following any inevitable steps, has he?

Rita   No.

Frank   There's no particular flaw in his character that has dictated his end. If he'd been warned of the consequences of standing beneath that particular tree he wouldn't have done it, would he? Understand?

Rita   So . . . so Macbeth brings it on himself?

Frank   Yes! You see, he goes blindly on and on and with every step he's spinning one more piece of thread which will eventually make up the network of his own tragedy. You see that?

Rita   I think so. I'm not used to thinkin' like this.

Frank   It's quite easy, Rita.

Rita   It is for you. I just thought it was a dead excitin' story. But the way you tell it you make me see all sorts of things in it. It's fun, tragedy, isn't it? (*She indicates the window and beyond.*) All them out there. They know all about that sort of thing, don't they?

Frank   Look, what are you doing for lunch?

Rita (*heading for the door*)   Lunch? Christ – me customer. She only wanted lo' lites – she'll come out looking like she's got fuckin' laser lights! (*She turns back.*) Ey, Frank, listen – I was thinkin' of goin' to the art gallery tomorrow. It's me half day off. D' y' wanna come with me?

Frank   All right. (*Beat.*) And – look, what are you doing on Saturday?

Rita   I work.

Frank   Well, when you finish work?

Rita   Dunno.

Frank   I want you to come over to the house.

Rita   Why?

Frank   Julia's organised a few people to come round for dinner.

Rita   An' y' want *me* to come?

Frank   Yes.

Rita   Why?

Frank   Why do you think?

Rita   I don't know.

Frank   Because you might *enjoy* it.

Rita   Oh.

Frank   Will you come?

Rita   If y' want.

Frank   What do *you* want?

Rita   All right, I'll come.

Frank   Will you bring Denny?

Rita   I don't know if he'll come.

Frank   Well, ask him!

Rita   All right.

Frank   What's wrong?

Rita   What shall I wear?

Blackout.

Scene Six

Frank   Now I don't mind: two empty seats at the dinner table means more of the vino for me. But Julia – Julia is the stage-manager type. If we're having eight people to dinner she expects to see eight. She likes order – probably why she took me on – it gives her a lot of practice – and having to cope with six instead of eight was extremely hard work on Julia. I'm not saying that *I* needed any sort of apology; you don't turn up, that's up to you, but . . .

Rita   I did apologise.

Frank   'Sorry couldn't come', scribbled on the back of your essay and thrust through the letter box? Rita, that's hardly an apology.

Rita   What does the word 'sorry' mean if it's not an apology? When I told Denny we were goin' to yours he went mad. We had a big fight about it.

Frank   I'm sorry. I didn't realise. But look, couldn't you have explained? Couldn't you have said that was the reason?

Rita   No. 'Cos that wasn't the reason. I told Denny if he wasn't gonna go I'd go on me own. An' I tried to. All day Saturday, all day in the shop I was thinkin' what to wear. Got home, tried on all kinds of dresses. Everythin' looked bleedin' awful. An' all the time I'm trying to think of things I can say, what I can talk about. An' I can't remember anythin'. It's all jumbled up in me head. I can't remember if it's Wilde who's witty an' Shaw who was Shavian or who the hell wrote *Howards End*.

Frank   Ogh Christ!

Rita   Then I got the wrong bus to your house. It took me ages to find it. Then I walked up your drive, an' I saw y' all through the window, you were sippin' drinks an' talkin' an' laughin'. An' I couldn't come in.

Frank   Of course you could.

Rita   I couldn't! I'd bought the wrong sort of wine. When I was in the off-licence I knew I was buyin' the wrong stuff. But I didn't know which was the right wine.

Frank   Rita, for Christ's sake; I wanted you to come along. You weren't expected to dress up or buy wine.

Rita   If you go out to dinner, don't you dress up? Don't you take wine?

Frank   Yes, but . . .

Rita   Well?

Frank   Well what?

Rita   Well, you wouldn't take sweet sparkling wine, would y'?

Frank   Does it matter what I do? It wouldn't have mattered if you'd walked in with a bottle of Spanish plonk.

Rita It *was* Spanish.

Frank Why couldn't you relax? It wasn't a fancy dress party. You could have come as yourself. Don't you realise how people would have seen you if you'd just – just breezed in? Mm? They would have seen someone who's funny, delightful, charming . . .

Rita But I don't want to be charming and delightful; *funny*, what's *funny*? I don't want to be *funny*. I wanna talk seriously with the rest of you, I don't wanna spend the night takin' the piss, comin' on with the funnies because that's the only way I can get into the conversation. I didn't want to come to your house just to play the court jester.

Frank You weren't being asked to play that role. I just – just wanted you to be yourself.

Rita But I don't want to be myself. Me? What's me? Some stupid woman who gives us all a laugh because she thinks she can learn, because she thinks that one day she'll be like the rest of them, talking seriously, confidently, with knowledge, live a civilised life. Well, she can't be like that really but bring her in because she's good for a laugh.

Frank (*erupting*) If you believe that that's why you were invited, to be laughed at, then you can get out of here right now. You were invited because I wished to have your company and if you can't believe that then I suggest you stop visiting me and start visiting an analyst who can cope with matters such as paranoia.

Rita I'm all right with you, here in this room; but when I saw those people you were with I couldn't come in. I would have seized up. Because I'm a freak. I can't talk to the people I live with any more. An' I can't talk to the likes of them on Saturday, or them out there, because I can't learn the language. I'm an alien. I went back to the pub where Denny was, an' me mother, an' our Sandra, an' her mates. I'd decided I wasn't comin' here again. I went into the pub an' they were singin', all of them singin' some song they'd learnt from the juke-box. An' I stood in that pub an' thought, just what in the name of Christ am I trying to do? Why don't I just pack it in, stay with them, an' join in with the singin'?

Frank   And why don't you?

Rita   You think I can, don't you? Just because you pass a pub doorway an' hear the singin' you think we're all OK, that we're all survivin', with the spirit intact. Well, I *did* join in with the singin', I didn't ask any questions, I just went along with it. But when I looked round, my mother had stopped singin', an' she was cryin'. Everyone just said she was pissed an' we should get her home. So we did, an' on the way I asked her why. I said, 'Why are y' cryin', Mother?' She said, 'Because – because we could sing better songs than those.' Ten minutes later, Denny had her laughing and singing again, pretending she hadn't said it. But she had. And that's why I came back. And that's why I'm staying.

Blackout.

Scene Seven

Frank *is absorbed in marking some papers.*

When **Rita** *enters, she is carrying a large holdall.*

Frank   One second. (*He finishes marking, looks up and sees the holdall.*) What's that?

Rita (*struggling to control herself throughout the following*)   It's my bag. My things.

Frank   Where are you going?

Rita   My mother's.

Frank   What's wrong? Rita.

Rita I got home from work, he'd packed my bag. He said either I stop comin' here an' come off the pill or I could get out altogether.

Frank Ogh . . . fuck.

Rita It was an ultimatum. I explained to him. I didn't get angry or anythin', I just explained to him how I *had* to do this. But he said it's warped me. He said I'd betrayed him. I suppose I have.

Frank *How* have you betrayed anyone?

Rita I have. I know he's right. But I couldn't betray meself. He says there's a time for education. An' it's not when y' twenty-six an' married.

Frank Where are you going to stay?

Rita I phoned me mother; she said I could go there for a week. Then I'll get a flat. I'm sorry, it's just . . . (*Although still struggling fiercely to deny her tears she momentarily loses the battle.*)

Frank Look, come on, sit down.

Refusing to be comforted, **Rita** *moves away to the window.*

Rita It's all right – I'll be OK. Just . . . just give me a minute. (*She turns back. Although the tears are now flowing she will not give in to them.*) What was me *Macbeth* essay like?

Frank Oh, sod *Macbeth*.

Rita Why?

Frank Rita!

Rita No, come on, come on, I want y' to tell me what you thought about it.

Frank Rita, in the circumstances I really . . .

Rita It doesn't matter, it doesn't! In the circumstances I need to go on, to talk about it an' do it. What was it like? I told y' it was no good. Is it really useless?

Frank   I – I really don't know what to say.

Rita   Well, try an' think of somethin'. Go on, I don't mind if y' tell me it was rubbish. I don't want pity, Frank. Was it rubbish?

Frank   No, no. Not rubbish. (*He picks up the papers he was marking earlier.*) It's a totally honest, passionate account of your reaction to a play. It's an unashamedly emotional statement about a particular experience.

Rita   Sentimental?

Frank   No no. It's far too honest for that. It's almost – erm – moving. But in terms of what you're asking me to teach you of passing exams . . . Oh, God, you see, I don't . . .

Rita   Say it, go on, say it!

Frank   In those terms it's worthless. It shouldn't be, but it is; in its own terms it's – it's wonderful.

Rita   It's worthless! You said. An' if it's worthless you've got to tell me because I want t' write essays like those on there. I want to know, an' pass exams like they do.

Frank   But if you're going to write this sort of stuff you're going to have to change.

Rita   All right. Tell me how to do it.

Frank   But I don't know if I want to tell you, Rita, I don't know that I want to teach you. What you already have is valuable.

Rita   Valuable? What's valuable? The only thing I value is here, comin' here once a week.

Frank   But, don't you see, if you're going to write this sort of thing – to pass examinations, you're going to have to suppress . . . perhaps even abandon your uniqueness. I'm going to have to change you.

Rita   But don't you realise, I *want* to change! Listen, is this your way of tellin' me that I can't do it? That I'm no good?

Frank   It's not that at –

Rita   If that's what you're tryin' to tell me I'll go now –

Frank   No no no. Of course you're good enough.

Rita   See, I know it's difficult for y' with someone like me. But you've just gorra keep tellin' me an' then I'll start to take it in; y'see, with me you've got to be dead firm. You won't hurt me feelings, y' know. If I do somethin' that's crap, I don't want pity, you just tell me, 'That's crap.' Here, it's crap. Right. So we dump that in the bin, an' we start again. (*She sits on the chair centre right.*)

Blackout.

Act Two

Scene One

Frank *is sitting at his desk typing. He pauses, takes a sip from the mug at his side, looks at his watch and then continues typing.*

Rita *bursts through the door. She is dressed in 'new', secondhand clothes.*

Rita   Frank! (*She twirls to show off her new clothes.*)

Frank (*smiling*)   And what is this vision, returning from the city? (*He gets up and moves towards* **Rita**.) Welcome back.

Rita   Frank, it was fantastic. (*She takes off her shawl and gives it to* **Frank**.)

He hangs it on the hook by the door. **Rita** *goes to the desk.*

Rita (*putting down her bag on the desk*)   Honest, it was – ogh!

Frank   What are you talking about, London or summer school?

Rita   Both. A crowd of us stuck together all week. We had a great time: dead late every night, we stayed up talkin', we went all round London, got drunk, went to the theatres, bought all sorts of secondhand gear in the markets . . . Ogh, it was . . .

Frank   So you won't have had time to do any actual work there?

Rita   Work? We never stopped. Lashin' us with it they were; another essay, lash, do it again, lash.

Frank *moves towards the desk.*

Rita   Another lecture, smack. It was dead good though. (*She goes and perches on the bookcase.*)

Frank *sits in the swivel chair, facing her.*

Rita Y' know at first I was dead scared. I didn't know anyone. I was gonna come home. But the first afternoon I was standin' in the library, y' know, lookin' at the books, pretendin' I was dead clever. Anyway, this tutor comes up to me, he looked at the book in me hand an' he said, 'Ah, are you fond of Ferlinghetti?' It was right on the tip of me tongue to say, 'Only when it's served with Parmesan cheese', but, Frank, I didn't. I held it back an' I heard meself sayin', 'Actually, I'm not too familiar with the American poets.' Frank, you woulda been dead proud of me. He started talkin' to me about the Beat poets – we sat around for ages – an' he wasn't even one of my official tutors, y' know. We had to go to this big hall for a lecture, there must have been two thousand of us in there. After he'd finished his lecture this professor asked if anyone had a question, an', Frank, I stood up! (*She stands.*) Honest to God, I stood up, an' everyone's lookin' at me. I don't know what possessed me, I was gonna sit down again, but two thousand people had seen me stand up, so I did it, I asked him the question.

There is a pause and **Frank** *waits.*

Frank Well?

Rita Well what?

Frank What was the question?

Rita Oh, I dunno, I forget now, 'cos after that I was askin' questions all week, y' couldn't keep me down. I think that first question was about Chekhov; 'cos y' know I'm dead familiar with Chekhov now.

He smiles, **Rita** *moves to the chair by the desk and sits.* **Frank** *swivels round to face her.*

Rita Hey, what was France like? Go on, tell us all about it.

Frank There isn't a lot to tell.

Rita   Ah, go on, tell me about it; I've never been to France. Tell me what it was like.

Frank   Well – it was rather hot . . . I've brought you back something. (*He hands her a duty-free pack of 200 Gauloise cigarettes.*)

Rita   I've packed it in. Did y' do much drinkin' over there?

Frank   Ah – a little. (*He puts the cigarettes on the table.*)

Rita   Tch. Did y' write?

Frank   A little.

Rita   Will y' show it to me?

Frank   Perhaps . . . One day, perhaps.

Rita   So y' wrote a bit an y' drank a bit? Is that all?

Frank (*in a matter-of-fact way*)   Julia left me.

Rita   What?

Frank   Yes. But not because of the obvious, oh no – it had nothing whatsoever to do with the ratatouille. It was actually caused by something called *oeufs en cocotte*.

Rita   What?

Frank   Eggs, my dear, eggs. Nature in her wisdom, cursed me with a dislike for the egg, be it *cocotte*, Florentine, Benedict or plain hard-boiled. Julia insisted that nature was wrong. I defended nature and Julia left.

Rita   Because of eggs?

Frank   Well – let's say that it began with eggs. (*He packs away the typewriter.*) Anyway, that's most of what happened in France. But now the holiday's over, you're back, even Julia's back.

Rita   Is she? Is she all right?

Frank (*putting the typewriter on the window desk and the sheets of paper in the top left drawer*)   Perfect. I get the feeling we shall be together for ever; or until she discovers *oeufs à la crécy*.

Rita   *Oeufs à la crécy?* Does that mean eggs? Trish was goin' on about those; is that all it is, eggs?

Frank   Trish?

Rita   Trish, me flatmate, Trish. God, is it that long since I've seen y', Frank? She moved into the flat with me just before I went to summer school.

Frank   Ah. Is she a good flatmate?

Rita   She's great. Y' know she's dead classy. Y' know, like she's got taste, y' know, like you, Frank, she's just got it. Everything in the flat's dead unpretentious, just books an' plants everywhere. D' y' know somethin', Frank? I'm havin' the time of me life; I am, you know. I even feel – (*She moves to the window.*) – I feel young, you know, like them down there.

Frank   My dear, twenty-six is hardly old.

Rita   I know that; but I mean, I feel young like them . . . I can be young. (*She goes to her bag.*) Oh, listen. (*She puts the bag on the desk and rummages in it, producing a box.*) Frank, I got you a present – it isn't much but I thought . . . (*She gives him a small box.*) Here.

Frank *puts on his glasses, gets the scissors out of the pot on the desk, cuts the string and opens the box to reveal an expensive pen.*

Rita   See what it says – it's engraved.

Frank (*reading*)   'Must only be used for poetry. By strictest order – Rita' . . . (*He looks at her.*)

Rita   I thought it'd be like a gentle hint.

Frank   Gentle?

Rita   Every time y' try an' write a letter or a note with that pen . . . it won't work; you'll read the inscription an' it'll make you feel dead guilty – 'cos y' not writing poetry. (*She smiles at him.*)

Frank (*getting up and pecking her on the cheek*)   Thank you – Rita. (*He sits down again.*)

Rita   It's a pleasure. Come on. (*She claps her hands.*) What are we doin' this term? Let's do a dead good poet. Come on, let's go an' have the tutorial down there.

Frank (*appalled*)   Down where?

Rita (*getting her bag*)   Down there – on the grass – come on.

Frank   On the grass? Nobody sits out there at this time of year.

Rita   They do – (*Looking out of the window.*) – there's some of them out there now.

Frank   Well, they'll have wet bums.

Rita   What's a wet bum? You can sit on a bench. (*She tries to pull him to his feet.*) Come on.

Frank (*remaining sitting*)   Rita, I absolutely protest.

Rita   Why?

Frank   Like Dracula. I have an aversion to sunlight.

Rita   Tch. (*She sighs.*) All right. (*She goes to the window.*) Let's open a window.

Frank   If you must open a window then go on, open it. (*He swivels round to watch her.*)

Rita (*struggling to open the window*)   It won't bleedin' budge.

Frank   I'm not surprised, my dear. It hasn't been opened for generations.

Rita (*abandoning it*)   Tch. Y' need air in here, Frank. The room needs airing. (*She goes and opens the door.*)

Frank   This room does not need air, thank you very much.

Rita   Course it does. A room is like a plant.

Frank   A room is like a plant?

Rita   Yeh, it needs air. (*She goes to her chair by the desk and sits.*)

Frank   And water, too, presumably? (*He gets up and closes the door.*) If you're going to make an analogy why don't we take it the whole way? Let's get a watering can and water the carpet; bring in two tons of soil and a bag of fertiliser. Maybe we could take cuttings and germinate other little rooms.

Rita   Go away, you're mental, you are.

Frank   You said it, distinctly, you said, a room is like a plant.

Rita   Well!

There is a pause.

Frank   Well what?

Rita   Well, any analogy will break down eventually.

Frank   Yes. And some will break down sooner than others. (*He smiles, goes to the bookcase and begins searching among the books.*) Look, come on . . . A great poet you wanted – we have one for you.

Rita *sits on the desk watching* **Frank**.

Frank   I was going to introduce you to him earlier.

As he rummages, a book falls to one side revealing a bottle of whisky which has been hidden behind it.

Now – where is he . . .?

Rita *goes over and picks the whisky bottle from the shelf.*

Rita   Are you still on this stuff?

Frank   Did I ever say I wasn't?

Rita (*putting the bottle down and moving away*)   No. But . . .

Frank   But what?

Rita   Why d' y' do it when y've got so much goin' for y', Frank?

Frank   It is indeed because I have 'so much goin' for me' that I do it. Life is such a rich and frantic whirl that I need the drink to help me step delicately through it.

Rita   It'll kill y', Frank.

Frank   Rita, I thought you weren't interested in reforming me.

Rita   I'm not. It's just . . .

Frank   What?

Rita   Just that I thought you'd start reforming yourself . . .

Frank   Under your influence?

She shrugs.

(*He stops searching and turns to face her.*) Yes. But Rita – if I repent and reform, what do I do when your influence is no longer here? What do I do when, in appalling sobriety, I watch you walk away and disappear, your influence gone for ever?

Rita   Who says I'm gonna disappear?

Frank   Oh you will, Rita. You've got to. (*He turns back to the shelves.*)

Rita   Why have I got to? This course could go on for years. An' when I've got through this one I might even get into the proper university here.

Frank   And we'll all live happily ever after? Your going is as inevitable as – as . . .

Rita   Macbeth?

Frank (*smiling*)   As tragedy, yes: but it will not be a tragedy, because I will be glad to see you go.

Rita   Tch. Thank you very much. (*She pauses.*) Will y' really?

Frank   Be glad to see you go? Well, I certainly don't want to see you stay in a room like this for the rest of your life. Now. (*He continues searching for the book.*)

Rita (*after a pause*)   You can be a real misery sometimes, can't y'? I was dead happy a minute ago an' then you start an' make me feel like I'm having a bad night in a mortuary.

Frank *finds the book he has been looking for and moves towards* **Rita** *with it.*

Frank   Well, here's something to cheer you up – here's our 'dead good' poet – Blake.

Rita   Blake? William Blake?

Frank   The man himself. *You* will understand Blake; they overcomplicate him, Rita, but you will understand – you'll love the man.

Rita   I know.

Frank   What? (*He opens the book.*) Look – look – read this . . . (*He hands her the book and then goes and sits in the swivel chair.*)

Rita *looks at the poem on the page indicated and then looks at* **Frank**.

Rita (*reciting from memory*)
'O Rose, thou art sick!
The invisible worm
That flies in the night,
In the howling storm,

Has found out thy bed
Of crimson joy
And his dark secret love
Does thy life destroy.'

Frank   You know it!

Rita (*laughing*)   Yeh. (*She tosses the book on the desk and perches on the bookcase.*) We did him at summer school.

Frank   Blake at summer school? You weren't supposed to do Blake at summer school, were you?

Rita   Nah. We had this lecturer though, he was a real Blake freak. He was on about it every day. Everythin' he said, honest, everything was related to Blake – he couldn't get his dinner in the refectory without relating it to Blake – Blake and Chips. He was good though. On the last day we brought him a present, an' on it we put that poem, y' know, 'The Sick Rose'. But we changed it about a bit; it was – erm –

'O Rose, thou aren't sick
Just mangled and dead
Since the rotten gardener
Pruned off thy head.'

We thought he might be narked but he wasn't, he loved it. He said – what was it? He said, 'Parody is merely a compliment masquerading as humour.'

Frank (*getting up and replacing the book on the shelf*)   So . . . you've already done Blake? You've covered all the *Songs of Innocence and Experience*?

Rita   Of course; you don't do Blake without doing *Innocence and Experience*, do y'?

Frank   No. Of course. (*He goes and sits in the swivel chair.*)

Blackout.

Rita *picks up her bag and shawl and exits.*

Scene Two

Frank *is sitting at his desk, marking an essay. Occasionally he makes a tutting sound and scribbles something. There is a knock at the door.*

Frank Come in.

Rita *enters, closes the door, goes to the desk and dumps her bag on it. She takes her chair and places it next to* **Frank** *and sits down.*

Rita (*in a peculiar voice*) Hallo, Frank.

Frank (*without looking up*) Hallo. Rita, you're late.

Rita I know, Frank, I'm terribly sorry. It was unavoidable.

Frank (*looking up*) Was it really? What's wrong with your voice?

Rita Nothing is wrong with it, Frank. I have merely decided to talk properly. As Trish says there is not a lot of point in discussing beautiful literature in an ugly voice.

Frank You haven't got an ugly voice; at least you *didn't* have. Talk properly.

Rita I am talking properly. I have to practise constantly, in everyday situations.

Frank You mean you're going to talk like that for the rest of this tutorial?

Rita Trish says that no matter how difficult I may find it I must persevere.

Frank Well, will you kindly tell Trish that I am not giving a tutorial to a parrot.

Rita I am not a parrot.

Frank (*appealingly*) Rita, stop it!

Rita But Frank, I have to persevere in order that I shall.

Frank Rita! Just be yourself.

Rita (*reverting to her normal voice*)   I am being myself. (*She gets up and moves the chair back to its usual place.*)

Frank   What's that?

Rita   What?

Frank   On your back.

Rita (*reaching up*)   Oh – it's grass.

Frank   Grass?

Rita   Yeh, I got here early today. I started talking to some students down on the lawn. (*She sits in her usual chair.*)

Frank   You were talking to students – down there?

Rita (*laughing*)   Don't sound so surprised. I can talk now, y' know, Frank.

Frank   I'm not surprised. Well! You used to be quite wary of them, didn't you?

Rita   God knows why. For students they don't half come out with some rubbish, y' know.

Frank   You're telling me?

Rita   I only got talking to them in the first place because as I was walking past I heard one of them sayin' as a novel he preferred *Lady Chatterley* to *Sons and Lovers*. I thought, I can keep walkin' and ignore it, or I can put him straight. So I put him straight. I walked over an' said, 'Excuse me but I couldn't help overhearin' the rubbish you were spoutin' about Lawrence.' Shoulda seen the faces on them, Frank. I said tryin' to compare *Chatterley* with *Sons and Lovers* is like tryin' to compare sparkling wine with champagne. The next thing is there's this heated discussion, with me right in the middle of it.

Frank   I thought you said the student claimed to 'prefer' *Chatterley* as a novel.

Rita   He did.

Frank So he wasn't actually suggesting that it was superior.

Rita Not at first – but then he did. He walked right into it . . .

Frank And you finished him off, did you, Rita?

Rita Frank, he was asking for it. He was an idiot. His argument just crumbled. It wasn't just me – everyone else agreed with me.

Frank *returns to reading the essay.*

Rita There was this really mad one with them; I've only been talkin' to them for five minutes and he's inviting me to go abroad with them all. They're all goin' to the South of France in the Christmas holidays, slummin' it.

Frank You can't go.

Rita What?

Frank You can't go – you've got your exams.

Rita My exams are before Christmas.

Frank Well – you've got your results to wait for . . .

Rita Tch. I couldn't go anyway.

Frank Why? (*He looks at her.*)

Rita It's all right for them. They *can* just jump into a bleedin' van an' go away. But I can't.

Frank *returns to the essay.*

Rita Tiger they call him, he's the mad one. His real name's Tyson but they call him Tiger.

Frank (*looking up*)   Is there any point me going on with this? (*He points to the essay.*)

Rita What?

Frank   Is there much point in working towards an examination if you're going to fall in love and set off for the South of –?

Rita (*shocked*)   What! Fall in love? With who? My God, Frank, I've just been talkin' to some students. I've heard of match-making but this is ridiculous.

Frank   All right, but please stop burbling on about Mr Tyson.

Rita   I haven't been burbling on.

He returns to the essay.

What's it like?

Frank   Oh – it – erm – wouldn't look out of place with these. (*He places it on top of a pile of other essays on his desk.*)

Rita   Honest?

Frank   Dead honest.

Blackout.

Frank *exits*.

Scene Three

Rita *is sitting in the armchair by the window, reading a heavy tome. There is the sound of muffled oaths from behind the door.*

Frank *enters, carrying his briefcase. He is very drunk.*

Frank   Sod them – no, fuck them! Fuck them, eh, Rita. (*He goes to the desk.*)

Rita   Who?

Frank   You'd tell them, wouldn't you? You'd tell them where to get off. (*He gets a bottle of whisky from his briefcase.*)

Rita   Tell who, Frank?

Frank Yes – students – students reported me! (*He goes to the bookcase and puts the whisky on the shelf.*) Me! Complained – you know something? They complained and it was the best lecture I've ever given.

Rita Were you pissed?

Frank Pissed? I was glorious! Fell off the rostrum twice. (*He comes round to the front of the desk.*)

Rita Will they sack you?

Frank (*lying flat on the floor*) The sack? God no, that would involve making a decision. Pissed is all right. To get the sack it'd have to be rape on a grand scale, and not just the students either.

Rita *gets up and moves across to look at him.*

Frank That would only amount to a slight misdemeanour. For dismissal it'd have to be nothing less than buggering the bursar . . . They suggested a sabbatical for a year – or ten . . . Europe – or America . . . I suggested that Australia might be more apt – the allusion was lost on them . . .

Rita Tch. Frank, you're mad. Even if y' don't think about yourself, what about the students?

Frank What about the students?

Rita Well, it's hardly fair on them if their lecturer's so pissed that he's falling off the rostrum. (*She goes to her chair by the desk and replaces the book in her bag.*)

Frank I might have fallen off, my dear, but I went down talking – and came up talking – never missed a syllable – what have they got to complain about?

Rita Maybe they did it for your own good.

Frank Or maybe they did it because they're a crowd of mealy-mouthed pricks who wouldn't know a poet if you beat them about the head with one. (*He half sits up.*)

'Assonance' – I said to them – 'Assonance means getting the rhyme wrong . . .' (*He collapses on the floor again.*) They looked at me as though I'd pissed on Wordsworth's tomb.

Rita Look, Frank, we'll talk about the Blake essay next week, eh?

Frank Where are you going? We've got a tutorial. (*He gets up and staggers towards her.*)

Rita Frank, you're not in any fit state for a tutorial. I'll leave it with y' an' we can talk about it next week, eh?

Frank No – no – you must stay – erm . . . Watch this – sober? (*He takes a huge breath and pulls himself together.*) Sober! Come on . . .

He takes hold of **Rita** *and pushes her round the desk and sits her in the swivel chair.*

Frank You can't go. I want to talk to you about this. (*He gets her essay and shows it to her.*) Rita, what's this?

Rita Is there something wrong with it?

Frank It's just, look, this passage about 'The Blossom' – you seem to assume that the poem is about sexuality.

Rita It is!

Frank Is it?

Rita Well, it's certainly like a richer poem, isn't it? If it's interpreted in that way.

Frank Richer? Why richer? We discussed it. The poem is a simple, uncomplicated piece about blossom, as if seen from a child's point of view.

Rita (*shrugging*) In one sense. But it's like, like the poem about the rose, isn't it? It becomes a more rewarding poem when you see that it works on a number of levels.

Frank Rita, 'The Blossom' is a simple, uncomplicated –

Rita   Yeh, that's what you say, Frank, but Trish and me and some others were talkin' the other night, about Blake, an' what came out of our discussion was that apart from the simple surface value of Blake's poetry there's always a like – erm – erm . . .

Frank   Well? Go on . . .

Rita (*managing to*)   . . . a like vein. Of concealed meaning. I mean if that poem's only about blossom then it's not much of a poem, is it?

Frank   So? You think it gains from being interpreted in this way?

Rita (*slightly defiantly*)   Is me essay wrong then, Frank?

Frank   It's not – not wrong. But I don't like it.

Rita   You're being subjective.

Frank (*half laughing*)   Yes – yes, I suppose I am. (*He goes slowly to the chair of the desk and sits down heavily.*)

Rita   If it was in an exam what sort of mark would it get?

Frank   A good one.

Rita   Well, what the hell are you sayin' then?

Frank (*shrugging*)   What I'm saying is that it's up to the minute, quite acceptable, trendy stuff about Blake; but there's nothing of you in there.

Rita   Or maybe, Frank, y' mean there's nothing of your views in there.

Frank (*after a pause*)   Maybe that is what I mean.

Rita   But when I first came to you, Frank, you didn't give me any views. You let me find my own.

Frank (*gently*)   And your views I still value. But, Rita, these aren't your views.

Rita   But you told me not to have a view. You told me to be objective, to consult recognised authorities. Well, that's what I've done. I've talked to other people, read other books an' after consultin' a wide variety of opinion I came up with those conclusions.

He looks at her.

Frank (*after a pause*)   Yes. All right.

Rita (*rattled*)   Look, Frank, I don't have to go along with your views on Blake, y' know. I can have a mind of my own, can't I?

Frank   I sincerely hope so, my dear.

Rita   And what's that supposed to mean?

Frank   It means – it means be careful.

Rita *jumps up and moves in towards* **Frank**.

Rita (*angrily*)   What d' y' mean be careful? I can look after myself. Just 'cos I'm learnin', just 'cos I can do it now an' read what I wanna read an' understand without havin' to come runnin' to you every five minutes y' start tellin' me to be careful. (*She paces about.*)

Frank   Because – because I care for you – I want you to care for yourself.

Rita   Tch. (*She goes right up to* **Frank**. *After a pause.*) I – I care for you, Frank . . . But you've got to – to leave me alone a bit. I'm not an idiot now, Frank – I don't need you to hold me hand as much . . . I can – I can do things on me own more now . . . And I am careful. I know what I'm doin'. Just don't – don't keep treatin' me as though I'm the same as when I first walked in here. I understand now, Frank; I know the difference between – between – Thomas Hardy and Rita Mae Brown. An' you're still treating me as though I'm hung up on *Rubyfruit Jungle*. (*She goes to the swivel chair and sits.*) Just . . . You understand, don't you, Frank?

Frank   Entirely, my dear.

Rita   I'm sorry.

Frank   Not at all. (*After a pause.*) I got round to reading it you know, *Rubyfruit Jungle*. It's excellent.

Rita (*laughing*)   Oh, go away, Frank. Of its type it's quite interesting. But it's hardly excellence.

Blackout.

Rita *exits.*

Scene Four

Frank *is sitting in the swivel chair.*

Rita *enters and goes to the desk.*

Rita   Frank . . .

He looks at his watch.

I know I'm late . . . I'm sorry.

He gets up and moves away.

Am I too late? We were talkin'. I didn't notice the time.

Frank   Talking?

Rita   Yeh. If it'll go in my favour we were talking about Shakespeare.

Frank   Yes . . . I'm sure you were.

Rita   Am I too late then? All right. I'll be on time next week, I promise.

Frank   Rita. Don't go.

Rita   No – honestly, Frank – I know I've wasted your time. I'll see y' next week, eh?

Frank   Rita! Sit down!

Rita *goes to her usual chair and sits.*

Frank (*going to the side of her*)   When you were so late I phoned the shop.

Rita   Which shop?

Frank   The hairdresser's shop. Where you work. Or, I should say, worked.

Rita   I haven't worked there for a long time. I work in a bistro now.

Frank   You didn't tell me.

Rita   Didn't I? I was telling someone.

Frank   It wasn't me.

Rita   Oh. Sorry.

Frank (*after a pause*)   It struck me that there was a time when you told me everything.

Rita   I thought I had told you.

Frank   No. Like a drink?

Rita   Who cares if I've left hairdressin' to work in a bistro?

Frank   I care. (*He goes to the bookshelves and takes a bottle from an eye-level shelf.*) You don't want a drink? Mind if I do?

Rita   But why do you care about details like that? It's just boring, insignificant detail.

Frank (*getting a mug from the small table*)   Oh. Is it?

Rita   That's why I couldn't stand being in a hairdresser's any longer: boring irrelevant detail all the time, on and on . . . Well, I'm sorry but I've had enough of that. I don't wanna talk about irrelevant rubbish any more.

Frank   And what do you talk about in your bistro? Cheers.

Rita   Everything.

Frank   Everything?

Rita   Yeh.

Frank   Ah.

Rita   We talk about what's important, Frank, and we leave out the boring details for those who want them.

Frank   Is Mr Tyson one of your customers?

Rita   A lot of the students come in; he's one of them. You're not gonna give me another warning, are y', Frank?

Frank   Would it do any good?

Rita   Look, for your information I do find Tiger fascinatin', like I find a lot of the people I mix with fascinating; they're young, and they're passionate about things that matter. They're not trapped – they're too young for that. And I like to be with them.

Frank (*moving and keeping his back to her*)   Perhaps – perhaps you don't want to waste your time coming here any more?

Rita   Don't be stupid. I'm sorry I was late. (*After a pause she gets up.*) Look, Frank, I've got to go. I'm meeting Trish at seven. We're going to see a production of *The Seagull*.

Frank   Yes. (*He turns to face her.*) Well. When Chekhov calls . . .

Rita   Tch.

Frank   You can hardly bear to spend a moment here, can you?

Rita (*moving towards him a little*)   That isn't true. It's just that I've got to go to the theatre.

Frank   And last week you didn't turn up at all. Just a phone call to say that you had to cancel.

Rita   It's just that – that there's so many things happening now. It's harder.

Frank   As I said, Rita, if you want to stop com—

Rita (*going right up to him*) For God's sake, I don't want to stop coming here. I've got to come here. What about my exam?

Frank Oh, I wouldn't worry about that. You'd sail through it anyway. You really don't have to put in the odd appearance out of sentimentality. (*He moves round to the other side of the desk.*) I'd rather you spared me that. (*He goes to drink.*)

Rita If you could stop pouring that junk down your throat in the hope that it'll make you feel like a poet you might be able to talk about things that matter instead of where I do or do not work, an' then it might be worth comin' here.

Frank Are you capable of recognising what does or does not matter, Rita?

Rita I understand literary criticism, Frank. When I come here that's what we're supposed to be dealing with.

Frank You want literary criticism? (*He looks at her for a moment and then goes to the top drawer of his desk and takes out two slim volumes and some typewritten sheets of poetry and hands them to her.*) I want an essay on that lot by next week.

Rita What is it?

Frank No sentimentality, no subjectivity. Just pure criticism. A critical assessment of a lesser-known English poet. Me.

Blackout.

Rita *exits.*

Scene Five

Frank *is sitting in a chair by the window desk with a mug in his hand and a bottle of whisky on the desk in front of him, listening to the radio. There is a knock at the door.*

Frank   Come in.

Rita *enters and goes to the swivel chair behind* **Frank***'s desk.*

Frank (*getting up and switching off the radio*)   What the – what the hell are you doing here? I'm not seeing you till next week.

Rita   Are you sober? Are you?

Frank   If you mean am I still this side of reasonable comprehension, then yes.

Rita (*going and standing next to him*)   Because I want you to hear this when you're sober. (*She produces his poems.*) These are brilliant, Frank, you've got to start writing again. (*She goes to the swivel chair and sits.*) This is brilliant. They're witty. They're profound. Full of style.

Frank (*going to the small table and putting down his mug*)   Ah . . . tell me again, and again.

Rita   They are, Frank. It isn't only me who thinks so. Me an' Trish sat up last night and read them. She agrees with me. Why did you stop writing? Why did you stop writing when you can produce work like this? We stayed up most of the night, just talking about it. At first we just saw it as contemporary poetry in its own right, you know, as somethin' particular to this century but look, Frank, what makes it more – more . . . What did Trish say –? More resonant than – purely contemperory poetry is that you can see in it a direct line through to nineteenth-century traditions of – of like wit an' classical allusion.

Frank (*going to the chair of the desk and standing by the side of it*)   Er – that's erm – that's marvellous, Rita. How fortunate I didn't let you see it earlier. Just think if I'd let you see it when you first came here.

Rita   I know . . . I wouldn't have understood it, Frank.

Frank   You would have thrown it across the room and dismissed it as a heap of shit, wouldn't you?

Rita (*laughing*)   I know . . . But I couldn't have understood it then, Frank, because I wouldn't have been able to recognise and understand the allusions.

Frank   Oh, I've done a fine job on you, haven't I?

Rita   It's true, Frank. I can see now.

Frank   You know, Rita, I think – I think that like you I shall change my name: from now on I shall insist upon being known as Mary, Mary Shelley – do you understand that allusion, Rita?

Rita   What?

Frank   She wrote a little Gothic number called *Frankenstein*.

Rita   So?

Frank   This – (*Picking up his poetry and moving round to* **Rita**.) – this clever, pyrotechnical pile of self-conscious allusion is worthless, talentless, shit and could be recognised as such by anyone with a shred of common sense. It's the sort of thing that gives publishing a bad name. Wit? You'll find more wit in the telephone book, and, probably, more insight. Its one advantage over the telephone directory is that it's easier to rip. (*He rips the poems up and throws the pieces on to the desk.*) It is pretentious, characterless and without style.

Rita   It's not.

Frank   Oh, I don't expect you to believe me, Rita; you recognise the hallmark of literature now, don't you? (*In a final gesture he throws a handful of the ripped pieces into the air and then goes to the chair and sits.*) Why don't you just go away? I don't think I can bear it any longer.

Rita   Can't bear what, Frank?

Frank   You, my dear – you . . .

Rita   I'll tell you what you can't bear, Mr Self-Pitying Piss-Artist: what you can't bear is that I am educated now.

What's up, Frank, don't y' like me now that the little girl's grown up, now that y' can no longer bounce me on Daddy's knee an' watch me stare back in wide-eyed wonder at everything he has to say? I'm educated, I've got what you have an' y' don't like it because you'd rather see me as the peasant I once was; you're like the rest of them – you like to keep your natives thick, because that way they still look charming and delightful. I don't need you. (*She gets up and picking up her bag moves away from the desk in the direction of the door.*) I know what clothes to wear, what wine to buy, what plays to see, what papers and books to read. I can do without you.

Frank   Is that all you wanted? Have you come all this way for so very, very little?

Rita   Oh, it's little to you, isn't it? It's little to you who squanders every opportunity and mocks and takes it for granted.

Frank   Found a culture have you, Rita? Found a better song to sing, have you? No – you've found a different song, that's all – and on your lips it's shrill and hollow and tuneless. Oh, Rita, Rita . . .

Rita   Rita? (*She laughs.*) Rita? Nobody calls me Rita but you. I dropped that pretentious crap as soon as I saw it for what it was. You stupid . . . Nobody calls me Rita.

Frank   What is it now then? Virginia?

Rita *exits, slamming the door.*

Or Charlotte? Or Jane? Or Emily? Virginia?

Blackout.

Scene Six

Frank *talking into the phone. He is leaning against the bookshelf. He is very drunk.*

Frank   Yes . . . I think she works there . . . Rita White.
No, no. Sorry . . . erm. What is it? Susan White? No? Thank
you . . . Thanks. (*He dials another number.*) Yes . . . Erm . . .
Trish, is it? . . . Erm, yes, I'm a friend of Rita's . . . I'm
sorry, Susan . . . Yes . . . could you just say that – erm – I've
. . . it's – erm – Frank here . . . her tutor . . . Yes . . . well,
could you tell her I've entered her for her examination . . .
Yes, you see she doesn't know the details . . . time and
where the exam is being held . . . Could you tell her to call
in? . . . Please . . . Yes . . . Thank you.

The lights fade to blackout.

Scene Seven

Rita *enters and shuts the door. She is wrapped in a large winter coat.
She lights a cigarette and moves across to a filing cabinet and places a
Christmas card with the others already there. She throws the envelope in
the waste-bin and opens the door, revealing* **Frank** *with a couple of
tea chests either side of him.*

*He is taken aback seeing her, and then he gathers himself and, picking
up one of the chests, enters the room.*

Rita *goes out to the corridor and brings in the other chest.* **Frank**
*gets the chair from the end of his desk and places it by the bookcase. He
stands on it and begins taking down the books from the shelves and
putting them into the chests.* **Rita** *watches him but he continues as if
she is not there.*

Rita   Merry Christmas, Frank. Have they sacked y'?

Frank   Not quite.

Rita   Well, why y' – packing your books away?

Frank   Australia. (*He pauses.*) Some weeks ago – made
rather a night of it.

Rita   Did y' bugger the bursar?

Frank   Metaphorically. And as it was metaphorical the sentence was reduced from the sack to two years in Australia. Hardly a reduction in sentence really – but . . .

Rita   What did Julia say?

Frank   *Bon voyage.*

Rita   She's not goin' with y'?

Frank *shakes his head.* **Rita** *begins helping him take down the books from the shelves and putting them in the chests.*

Rita   What y' gonna do?

Frank   What do you think I'll do? Aussie? It's a paradise for the likes of me.

Rita   Tch. Come on, Frank . . .

Frank   It is. Didn't you know the Australians named their favourite drink after a literary figure? Forster's Lager they call it. Of course they get the spelling wrong – rather like you once did!

Rita   Be serious.

Frank   For God's sake, why did you come back here?

Rita   I came to tell you you're a good teacher. (*After a pause.*) Thanks for enterin' me for the exam.

Frank   That's all right. I know how much it had come to mean to you.

Rita *perches on the small table while* **Frank** *continues to take books from the upper shelves.*

Rita   You didn't want me to take it, did y'? Eh? You woulda loved it if I'd written 'Frank knows all the answers' across me paper, wouldn't y'? I nearly did an' all. When the invigilator said, 'Begin', I turned over me paper with the rest of them, and while they were all scribbling away against the clock, I just sat there, lookin' at the first question. Y' know what it was, Frank? 'Suggest ways in which one might cope with some of the staging difficulties in a production of *Peer Gynt*.'

Frank *gets down, sits on the chair and continues to pack the books.*

Frank   Well, you should have had no trouble with that.

Rita   I did though. I just sat lookin' at the paper an' thinkin' about what you'd said. I tried to ignore it, to pretend that you were wrong. You think you gave me nothing, did nothing for me. You think I just ended up with a load of quotes an' empty phrases; an' I did. But that wasn't your doin'. I was so hungry. I wanted it all so much that I didn't want it to be questioned. I told y' I was stupid. It's like Trish, y' know me flatmate. I thought she was so cool an' together – I came home the other night an' she'd tried to top herself. What's all that about? She spends half her life eatin' wholefoods an' health foods to make her live longer an' the other half tryin' to kill herself. (*She pauses.*) I sat lookin' at the question, an' thinkin' about it all. Then I picked up me pen an' started.

Frank   And you wrote, 'Do it on the radio'?

Rita   I could have done. An' you'd have been proud of me if I'd done that an' rushed back to tell you – wouldn't y'? But I chose not to. I had a choice. I did the exam.

Frank   I know. A good pass as well.

Rita   Yeh. An' it might be worthless in the end. But I had a choice. I chose, me. Because of what you'd given me. I had a choice. I wanted to come back an' tell y' that. That y' a good teacher.

Frank (*stopping working and looking at her*)   You know – erm – I hear very good things about Australia. The thing is, why don't you – come as well?

Rita   Isn't that called jumpin' a sinkin' ship?

Frank   So what? Do you really think there's any chance of keeping it afloat?

She looks at him and then at the shelves.

Rita (*seeing the empty whisky bottles*) 'Ey, Frank, what's it like havin' your own bottle bank?

Frank (*smiling*) You're being evasive.

Rita (*going and sitting on a tea chest*) I know. Tiger's asked me to go down to France with his mob.

Frank Will you?

Rita I dunno. He's a bit of a wanker really. But I've never been to France. An' me mother's invited me to hers for Christmas.

Frank What are you going to do?

Rita I dunno. I might go to France. I might go to me mother's. I might even have a baby. I dunno. I'll make a decision, I'll choose. I dunno.

Frank *has found a package hidden behind some of the books. He takes it down.*

Frank Whatever you do, you might as well take this . . .

Rita What?

Frank (*handing it to her*) It's erm – well it's er – it's a dress really. I bought it some time ago – for erm – for an educated woman friend – of mine . . .

Rita *takes the dress from the bag.*

Frank I erm – don't – know if it fits, I was rather pissed when I bought it . . .

Rita An educated woman, Frank? An' this is what you call a scholarly neckline?

Frank When choosing it I put rather more emphasis on the word woman than the word educated.

Rita All I've ever done is take from you. I've never given anything.

Frank   That's not true, you've –

Rita   It is true. I never thought there was anythin' I could give you. But there is. Come here, Frank . . .

Frank   What?

Rita   Come here . . . (*She pulls out a chair.*) Sit on that . . .

Frank *is bewildered.*

Rita   Sit . . .

Frank *sits and* **Rita**, *eventually finding a pair of scissors on the desk, waves them in the air.*

Rita   I'm gonna take ten years off you . . . (*She goes across to him and begins to cut his hair.*)

Blackout.

Notes

Act One
Scene One

1 *Eliot:* Thomas Stearns Eliot (1888–1965), American-
   born poet, playwright and essayist, whose poetry
   includes *The Waste Land* (1922) and *Four Quartets*
   (1936–42). After his marriage to Vivienne Haigh-Wood
   in 1915, Eliot spent most of his life in England. He
   became a British citizen in 1927.

1 *Emerson:* Ralph Waldo Emerson (1803–82), American
   essayist, philosopher and poet.

1 *Euripides:* together with Sophocles and Aeschylus,
   Euripides (*c.*480–*c.*406 BC) is one of the three great
   ancient Greek writers of tragedy. Euripides' plays
   include *Medea, Hecuba* and *The Trojan Women,* all of
   which have central and strong female roles. The
   significance of Eliot, Emerson and Euripides is that
   Frank is working his way along the row of books from
   left to right. His books are organised in alphabetical
   order and he is searching for his whisky bottle in the 'E'
   section of his library.

1 *Eureka:* 'I have found it!' in Greek. Archimedes, the
   ancient Greek philosopher and mathematician, is said
   to have shouted 'Eureka!' when he made a discovery in
   his bath. Frank has found the solution to his problem
   and now moves back along the shelf or up a shelf to the
   books whose authors' name begins with the letter 'D'.

1 *Dickens:* Charles Dickens (1812–70), the great Victorian
   novelist who first made his name in 1836 with *Pickwick
   Papers.* Most of his novels were originally published in
   instalments and when collected into book form they
   make relatively lengthy and thick volumes. The

editions of Dickens that Frank has on his shelf are
obviously the ideal shape and size behind which to
conceal bottles of whisky.

1   *Open University*: the idea of a 'university of the air', using
radio and television to prepare students for degrees,
was developed by Jennie Lee, a minister in Harold
Wilson's Labour government of 1964. Serious planning
for an Open University began in September 1967 and
Professor Walter Perry was appointed as the first Vice-
Chancellor. By September 1969, building of new
premises in Milton Keynes was under way and students
started applying for the proposed undergraduate
courses during 1970. The first teaching of Open
University students took place from January 1971. By
the time of the premiere of *Educating Rita* (1980) there
were some 70,000 students taking OU courses with
around 6,000 graduates achieving honours degrees
each year. The majority of the teaching and learning
on Open University courses is through the use of
distance-learning materials linked to radio and/or
television programmes. This is supplemented with
seminars and tutorials organised in regional centres
and by attendance at a summer school. Increasingly
much of the tutoring is now carried out through on-line
learning and e-learning materials. Willy Russell has
taken a measure of artistic licence in giving Rita far
more tutor-contact time than would normally be the
case for an Open University student.

1   *Henry James*: the novelist (1843–1916), whose books
include *Daisy Miller* (1879), *Portrait of a Lady* (1881) and
The Bostonians (1886). Henry James was born in New
York, spent his early years travelling around Europe
and finally settled in England. He became a British
citizen in 1915.

1   *Thomas Hardy*: the Dorset-born novelist and poet
(1840–1928), whose novels are played out against the
rural backdrop of his fictional Wessex.

2   *ratatouille*: a French vegetable dish made from
aubergines, courgettes, onions, peppers and tomatoes,

seasoned with garlic and basil. Contrary to Frank's statement that it is impossible to overcook ratatouille, the vegetables should not be allowed to go mushy.

2   *napalm*: a liquid used in flame-throwers and incendiary bombs.

2   *Sotto voce*: an Italian phrase which literally means 'under the voice'. Frank is saying 'four [pints]' to himself so that the audience hears it but Julia cannot hear it at the other end of the telephone.

3   *fascinated as much as he is fazed by her*: this stage direction has been added to the 2003 edition of the play. The word 'fazed' suggests that Frank is thrown by Rita's presence and behaviour and has lost some of his usual composure.

4   *dead surprised*: Rita uses the word 'dead' as a Liverpudlian (Scouse) dialect word to mean 'really' or 'very'. There are numerous examples of it throughout the play: 'Y' dead impressive when you're angry' (p. 28); 'pretendin' I was dead clever' (p. 55). Frank also uses the word as an affectionate turn of phrase, 'Dead honest' (p. 66).

4   *extracurricular*: work outside the normal university timetable. Frank is taking on the Open University tuition in addition to the teaching and responsibilities of his full-time job as a university lecturer.

4   *bona fide*: Latin phrase that translates as 'in good faith'. Here Frank is using it in the sense of being a genuine or real lecturer.

5   *wacky backy*: colloquial expression for smoking cannabis. Literally, tobacco (backy) that causes unpredictable (wacky) behaviour.

5   *Dylan Thomas*: Welsh writer (1914–53), best known for *Under Milk Wood*, his radio play. Frank is referring to Thomas's poem 'Do Not Go Gentle into that Good Night' written after the death of his father. The poem declares that 'Old age should burn and rave at close of day'. Frank immediately thinks of a 'literary' poet whereas Rita is referring to the popular Roger McGough, of whom Frank has never heard.

5   *Roger McGough*: Liverpudlian poet, performer and
     broadcaster (born 1937). He first came to prominence
     with the publication of *The Mersey Sound* (1967), a best-
     selling collection of poems by Roger McGough and
     fellow Liverpool poets, Adrian Henri and Brian Patten.
     Rita is referring to a poem called 'Funny sort of bloke'
     (1979), where the old man screams, 'Come out Death
     and fight' (Roger McGough, *Collected Poems*, Penguin,
     2004, p. 256). Roger McGough also wrote a poem
     dedicated to Willy Russell entitled *Educating Rita* (1982)
     (see *Collected Poems*, p. 289).

6   *Faulkner*: William Faulkner (1897–1962), Mississippi-
     born American writer who won the Nobel Prize for
     Literature in 1950. He is considered to be one of the
     great writers of American fiction but he never
     graduated from high school or completed his university
     degree. He first came to prominence with *The Sound and
     the Fury* (1929) and is perhaps best known for the novel
     As I Lay Dying (1930). Having previously got to the end
     of the 'E' section in his library with Euripides, Frank
     has now moved further along to authors whose
     surname begins with 'F'.

6   *Fielding*: Henry Fielding (1707–54), English dramatist
     and novelist best known for his bawdy tale *Tom Jones*
     (1749).

6   *Forster*: E. (Edward) M. (Morgan) Forster (1879–1970),
     English novelist, essayist and broadcaster. Forster wrote
     six novels, including *A Room with a View* and *A Passage to
     India*. His homosexuality was kept from public
     knowledge during his lifetime. His novel *Maurice*, an
     explicit homosexual love story, was written in 1913/14
     but not published until 1971.

7   *Howards End*: E. M. Forster's fourth novel, published in
     1910. It deals with three different groups belonging to
     the Edwardian middle classes. Leonard and Jacky Bast
     represent the lower middle class trying to better
     themselves through education and hard work; the
     Schlegels are cultured middle-class bohemian
     intellectuals and the Wilcoxes are wealthy middle-class

business people. The motto of the novel is the phrase 'only connect'. This is Forster's attempt to bring together within upper-middle-class English society the disparate worlds of the emotional and cultured (personified in the character of Helen Schlegel) and the practical and materialistic as portrayed in the character Henry Wilcox.

8   *effin' and blinding*: swearing and cursing. There is the obvious 'f' word which Rita goes on to use and a considerable number of swear words and blasphemies begin with 'b'. 'Blinding' probably comes from an old blasphemy, 'God blind me'. Rita goes on to use her own 'b' word.

8   *grouse*: a game bird, traditionally bred on country estates for the express purpose of being shot by the aristocracy and the landed gentry.

10   *Assonance*: the way words are used in poetry when either the vowel sounds are the same but the consonants differ (e.g. time/light) or when the consonants are the same but the vowel sounds differ (e.g. mystery/mastery). A rhyme is where what is called the 'terminal sounds' of words are the same (e.g. bank/frank). Rita's definition of assonance as 'gettin' the rhyme wrong' is a down-to-earth way of describing it that Frank later tells her he has used in one of his lectures.

10   *Yeats*: W. (William) B. (Butler) Yeats (1865–1939), Irish Protestant poet and playwright and founder of the Irish National Theatre Company based at the Abbey Theatre in Dublin.

10   *The wine lodge*: Rita thinks that Frank is referring to 'Yates' which sounds the same as Yeats. Yates's is a UK pub chain with over fifty branches nationwide. There are three in Liverpool. In the 1970s/80s they were known as Yates Wine Lodge but in recent years they have moved more upmarket and have been rebranded as Yates's.

10   *'The Wild Swans at Coole'*: this is the title poem of a collection that Yeats published in 1919. Each of the

five, six-line verses has a rhyme scheme of ABCBDD.
The first verse is the only one ending with an assonant
rhyming couplet.

11 *Rita Mae Brown*: acclaimed American novelist, poet,
feminist, humorist, activist, screenwriter, lesbian,
animal lover and farmer (born 1944). Gained some
notoriety as the one-time lover and partner of the
international tennis star, Martina Navratilova. Rita
Mae Brown has written some twenty books to date,
including an autobiography entitled *Rita Will: Memoir of
a Literary Rabble-Rouser*. She has written several
humorous books with her feline companion, Sneaky
Pie Brown, giving them titles such as *Murder, She
Meowed* and *Claws and Effect*.

11 *Rubyfruit Jungle*: Rita Mae Brown's first novel published
in 1973. It is essentially a 'coming-of-age novel' about a
teenage girl called Molly Bolt and deals with her
coming out as a lesbian. The title comes from the
following interchange in the novel:

> [Molly:] 'When I make love to women I think of their genitals
> as a, as a ruby fruit jungle.'
> [Polina:] 'Ruby fruit jungle?'
> 'Yeah, women are thick and rich and full of hidden treasures
> and besides that, they taste good.' (p. 203)

11 *wanna lend it*: Scouse dialect meaning 'Would you like to
borrow it?'

12 *Eliot Ness*: American law enforcement agent. Eliot Ness
(1903–57) was responsible for the conviction of the
notorious mobster Al Capone during the prohibition
period in late 1920s, early 1930s Chicago. His team of
agents became known as the Untouchables, which was
also the title of his autobiography and the television
series starring Robert Stack made in the late 1950s. A
film of *The Untouchables*, starring Kevin Costner as Eliot
Ness and directed by Brian de Palma was released in
1987. Frank confuses Eliot with T. S. Eliot, the poet
(see note to page 1).

12 *J. Arthur Prufrock*: Rita is referring to Eliot's poem, 'The

Love Song of J. Alfred Prufrock', from his first
published collection of poetry, *Prufrock and Other
Observations* (1917). The lewd joke that followed this line
in the 1980 version of the script has been cut in the
revised version. Originally Frank corrects Rita:

> **Frank**   I think you'll find it was 'J. Alfred Prufock', Rita. J.
> Arthur is something else altogether.
> **Rita**   Oh yeh. I never thought of that.

J. Arthur Rank created his own film-making and
distribution company in England during the 1930s and
it remained in existence for over fifty years. Ironically,
the famous gong logo can be seen on the original prints
of the film version of *Educating Rita* because the Rank
Organisation was the distributor of the film in the UK
on its first release. The Rank Organisation no longer
exists which is why the joke has dated. A 'J. Arthur' is
rhyming slang for 'a wank'. This joke has been
replaced with a similar joke earlier in the scene when
Rita suggests the 'wink/wank' combination as an
example of assonance.

13   *never crack on*: Scouse phrase meaning 'they'll never let
you know or tell you'.

13   *come the hairdresser's*: one of the rare occasions in the
script where the spoken Scouse dialect is captured by
omitting the word 'to'. 'That's why people come to the
hairdresser's'.

14   *Formby*: originally a small coastal village which grew
into a commuter town after the coming of the railway
in 1847. It is thirteen miles north of Liverpool.

14   *Southport*: Southport is a seaside resort seven miles
further up the coast from Formby. Frank's response,
'up towards Southport', makes Rita realise that he lives
in Formby, the place she has just described as 'a hole'.
In the 1980 version of the script the dialogue is less
subtle:

> **Rita**   I hate that hole, don't you?
> **Frank**   Yes.

Rita Where do you live?
Frank Formby.
Rita Oh.

16 *sun's gone over the yardarm*: a nautical term referring to the time of day when the sun would drop below the yardarm on a sailing ship. On ships crossing the North Atlantic ocean this occurs around mid-day when it is traditional for the crew to have a break and to take a drink. The yardarm is the pole which juts out from a ship's mast to support the sail.

16 *Guinness*: famous Irish stout originally brewed by Arthur Guinness in Dublin in the mid-eighteenth century. Known for its dark colour (almost black) and its distinctive white creamy head.

16 *Wilde*: Oscar Fingal O'Flahertie Wills Wilde (1854–1900), Irish poet, story-writer and playwright, known for his sharp wit and wonderful way with words. He became notorious in his lifetime for his homosexual relationship with Lord Alfred Douglas that led to two years' imprisonment for indecent sexual behaviour.

16 *Swift*: Jonathan Swift (1667–1745), Dublin-born writer particularly remembered as a prose satirist. Best known for *Gulliver's Travels* which first appeared in 1726.

17 *a geriatric hippy*: the hippy culture of the 1960s was an alternative lifestyle characterised by young people who had long and wild hairstyles. Rita is rudely implying that Frank is far too old to have long hair like a hippy.

Scene Two

18 *patina*: generally used in the antiques trade to refer to the surface texture that objects acquire over time.

19 *Eton or Harrow*: two famous British boys' 'public schools' (in effect, private schools) charging extremely high fees. Eton College, near Windsor in Berkshire, was founded by Henry VI in 1440 and is favoured by royalty and the aristocracy. Prince William and Prince Harry were both educated at Eton. Harrow School in North

London was founded in 1572 and has produced many
of Britain's Prime Ministers including Churchill. The
poet Byron and the playwright Sheridan were both
educated at Harrow.

19   *tuck shop and a matron and jolly hockey sticks*: the 'tuck shop'
in a public school supplies sweets and food. The
matron looks after the health and well-being of the
pupils in a public school. Hockey is a game associated
with private girls' schools. The image of tuck shops and
jolly hockey sticks is associated with girls' comics of the
60s and 70s like *Bunty* and the St Trinian's cartoons by
Ronald Searle. Girls from private boarding schools
were portrayed in gym-slips and straw boaters,
wielding hockey sticks and speaking in upper-class
accents.

19   *Jones Major an' Jones Minor*: in public schools pupils are
usually called by their surnames. Major and minor are
used to distinguish between older and younger brothers
or sisters respectively.

19   *Coppin' off*: Scouse expression meaning 'to get off with a
member of the opposite sex'.

20   *Jane Austin*: Jane Austen (1775–1817), English novelist
whose best-known work includes *Sense and Sensibility*
(1811), *Pride and Prejudice* (1813) and *Emma* (1816).

20   *Ethel Austen*: Ethel Austin started a clothes shop in 1934
in the front room of her terraced house in Liverpool.
Today it is a multi-million pound company with over
five hundred shops in the UK. The fact that Rita
mispronounces both Jane's and Ethel's surnames
suggests that it is deliberate.

21   *purely objective*: neutral, outside view based on given facts
rather than on personal opinion. More or less the
opposite of subjective.

21   *subjective*: giving a personal and therefore potentially
biased view based on one's own feelings and thoughts.

21   *sentimental*: given to reacting to things on an emotional
level. Frank is saying that if you let your feelings get in
the way you cannot be objective in your criticism.

21   *partial*: to have a particular liking for something or to be

biased towards something.

21 *partisan*: devoted to one particular cause or idea. To have a one-sided point of view.

21 *established literary critique*: a tradition that has been built up by academics and critics to write about literature.

22 *F. R. Leavis*: Frank Raymond Leavis (1895–1978) was instrumental in establishing a tradition and a place for serious literary criticism. He was born and educated in Cambridge. In 1932 he was appointed Director of English Studies at Downing College, Cambridge, and his entire working life was spent there. His best-known works are his volumes of criticism, *New Bearings in English Poetry* (1932) and *The Great Tradition* (1948).

22 *ivory tower*: distanced from real life, a sheltered and closeted existence.

23 *Marxist perspective*: a critical view based on the philosophical and economic ideas of the German philosopher, Karl Marx (1818–83). Marxism states that society could be influenced and changed by economic forces and that capitalism could be replaced by a classless society where wealth is distributed fairly for the good of the community rather than for the individual.

24 *Go 'way*: a Scouse version of the expression, 'get away with you'. In other words, 'you're having me on' or 'I don't believe you'.

24 *fire the muse*: possible reference to the opening of Shakespeare's *Henry the Fifth*:

> O for a muse of fire, that would ascend
> The brightest heaven of invention.

The phrase literally means 'to inspire me'. The Muses were nine sister-goddesses in Greek mythology who were identified with various arts and sciences. 'The muse' is traditionally called on by a poet to spur on (or fire up) his/her creative ideas.

28 *'only connect'*: see note on *Howards End* (page 86).

Scene Three

28   *Childwall*: an area of Liverpool, about four and a half
miles west of the city centre.

28   *he's just copped a couple of tickets*: Scouse dialect phrase
meaning, 'he's just got hold of two tickets'.

29   *Ibsen's Peer Gynt*: Henrik Ibsen (1828–1906), the
Norwegian playwright, is best known for his realist
dramas. *Peer Gynt* (1867) is a sprawling five-act symbolic
verse play that travels across the world and through
time. It is best remembered today for the incidental
music composed for the original production by Edvard
Grieg.

32   *culture in a pot of yoghurt*: the live bacteria that turns milk
into yoghurt are called 'the culture'.

Scene Four

35   *Oxbridge dons*: the teaching staff from Oxford or
Cambridge universities.

36   *Chekhov*: Anton Chekhov (1860–1904), Russian
playwright known for the detailed naturalism of his
plays.

37   *rockin' the coffin*: local expression meaning to change or
disturb things from the way they are.

37   *Everton an' Liverpool*: Liverpool has two world-class
football teams. Everton, known as 'The Blues', was
founded in 1878 and plays at Goodison Park.
Liverpool, known as 'The Reds', was founded in 1892
and plays at Anfield. Both football grounds are situated
three miles north of the city centre and are less than a
mile from each other.

39   *Constantin*: Constantin Trevlev, the young would-be
playwright in Chekhov's *The Seagull* (see below) who
shoots himself at the end of the play.

40   *MA*: Master of Arts: a postgraduate qualification
demonstrating a high level of specialist study.

41   *The Seagull*: a comedy in four acts by Anton Chekhov,
written in 1896. Constantin stages a play he has written
starring his girlfriend, Nina. The audience consists of

his mother, Arkadina, and her lover, the successful writer Trigorin, who are both critical of the play. Constantin kills a seagull that he lays at Nina's feet because he is losing her affections to Trigorin. The seagull becomes a symbol for the way Trigorin takes Nina as his lover and casually destroys her. When Nina tells the ever-faithful Constantin that she still loves Trigorin despite everything, Constantin goes out and shoots himself. As Rita says, what happens in the play is tragic but in Chekhov the term comedy is used to refer to the way in which the detailed and psychological nature of the characters is portrayed.

41   *The Importance of Bein'* . . . *what's-his-name*: *The Importance of Being Earnest* – Oscar Wilde's witty comedy, first produced in 1895. It contains the formidable character of Lady Bracknell who has such memorable lines as, 'To lose one parent may be regarded as a misfortune . . . to lose both seems like carelessness.'

Scene Five

43   *Out, out, brief candle!*: Rita is quoting from Act Five, Scene Five, of Shakespeare's *Macbeth*, from Macbeth's speech after he is told that Lady Macbeth is dead.

44   *Lo' lights*: low lights are a type of hair colouring. In order to give dyed hair a more natural look some strands of hair are coloured a slightly deeper shade than the overall colour.

Scene Six

48   *Shaw*: George Bernard Shaw (1856–1950), Irish-born critic, novelist and prolific playwright who won the Nobel Prize for Literature in 1925. *Pygmalion* (1912) is one of his best-known plays and has a similar theme to *Educating Rita* in that Professor Higgins educates the working-class Eliza Doolittle.

48   *if it's Wilde who's witty an' Shaw who was Shavian*: Rita has got this the right way around. Shavian is the term used

to refer to the style of writing by George Bernard Shaw (see previous note). Wilde wrote of Bernard Shaw, 'He hasn't an enemy in the world, and none of his friends like him.'

Act Two
Scene One

54   *summer school*: to give Open University students the opportunity to work with other students from across the country, there are a number of summer schools run for one or two weeks during the summer months. They are residential and often take place on university campuses while the full-time students are away.

55   *Ferlinghetti*: Lawrence Ferlinghetti (born 1919), American poet and artist who first came to prominence in the 1950s. In 1955, he co-founded the City Lights Bookshop in San Francisco which is still a meeting-place for writers and artists today. His collection *A Coney Island of the Mind* is one of the most popular poetry books in the United States.

55   *Parmesan cheese*: a hard Italian cheese which is grated over pasta dishes. On hearing the name Ferlinghetti, Rita immediately associates it with spaghetti Bolognese which is sprinkled with Parmesan cheese.

55   *the Beat poets*: the 'Beat Generation' was a term coined by the American writer Jack Kerouac in the early 1950s and is applied to a group of writers who were seen as being nonconformist. Ferlinghetti was part of this group and when he published fellow writer Allen Ginsberg's work *Howl* in 1956 he was arrested and charged with breaking obscenity laws.

56   *a duty-free pack of 200 Gauloise cigarettes*: at the time the play was written there were customs restrictions on the amount of cigarettes and alcohol that could be brought back into the UK from abroad without having to pay duty. The limit for cigarettes was 200. Gauloise is a distinctively French brand of cigarettes.

56   *cocotte, Florentine, Benedict*: different ways of cooking eggs.

Cocotte: eggs baked in the oven in individual dishes;
Florentine: eggs cooked with spinach; Benedict:
poached eggs served on a muffin, traditionally with
ham and hollandaise sauce.

57 *oeufs à la crécy*: eggs served on a *brioche* (a type of French
bread) with carrots and a cream sauce.

58 *Dracula*: the fictional creation of Bram Stoker
(1847–1912) first published in 1897, has become the
subject of innumerable horror movies. Count Dracula
lives for ever by sucking the blood out of the living. He
is a creature of the night and sunlight can destroy him.

59 *an analogy*: illustrating one thing (a room needing air) by
comparing it to another (a plant needing water).

60 *This course could go on for years*: there is no time limit for
obtaining an Open University degree, which is built up
from taking different modules of study. The average
time it takes for a BA degree is six years.

61 *Blake*: William Blake (1757–1827), Romantic visionary
artist and poet. Rita is quoting 'The Sick Rose' from
the collection *Songs of Experience* published in 1794.

Scene Two

64 *Lady Chatterley to Sons and Lovers*: two novels by D.
(David) H. (Herbert) Lawrence (1885–1930). *Sons and
Lovers* (1913) is a semi-autobiographical novel about a
sensitive boy growing up in working-class Nottingham.
Lady Chatterley's Lover (1928) was not published in the
UK until 1960. This led to an infamous obscenity trial
against Penguin Books because of explicit sex scenes
between the married upper-class Lady Chatterley and
her working-class gamekeeper, Mellors.

66 *burbling on*: Frank's choice of word here indicates a sense
of jealousy about the way that Rita is talking excitedly
about Tiger/Mr Tyson.

Scene Three

67 *the bursar*: the finance director in the more traditional

universities. The alliteration of 'buggering' and 'bursar'
creates a comic effect in the dialogue.

67 *a sabbatical*: in some universities it is common practice to
allow teaching staff to have up to a year's paid leave
from their duties to travel or to undertake further
study. It comes from the Jewish word, *sabbath,* meaning
the day of rest. The sabbath is traditionally a day of
worship when no one works.

67 *Australia*: Frank is alluding to the fact that during the
eighteenth and nineteenth centuries convicted prisoners
were transported to Australia as a punishment.

68 *Wordsworth*: William Wordsworth (1770–1850), English
Romantic poet, born in the Lake District. He was
made Poet Laureate in 1843. He is best known for
poetry that evokes the idyllic quality of the English
landscape.

68 *The Blossom*: a poem by William Blake from *Songs of
Innocence* (1789):

> Merry, merry sparrow!
> Under leaves so green
> A happy blossom
> Sees you, swift as arrow,
> Seek your cradle narrow,
> Near my bosom.

> Pretty, pretty robin!
> Under leaves so green
> A happy blossom
> Hears you sobbing, sobbing,
> Pretty, pretty robin,
> Near my bosom.

69 *simple surface value*: Rita mentions the poem working on a
number of levels. Literary criticism talks about the
denotative meaning of a poem which is the direct and
obvious interpretation of the words (the surface value)
and connotative meaning which is the possible
associations there might be beyond the literal meaning.
On one level this poem could just be about two garden
birds but on another there might be a reference to a

lover or a friend suggested by the line 'Near my
bosom', and the way the blossom is given the human
attributes of seeing and hearing.

70   *Thomas Hardy*: see note to page 1.

Scene Five

76   *Mary Shelley*: Mary Wollstonecraft Shelley (1797–1851)
wrote the Gothic horror novel *Frankenstein* when she
was nineteen and it was published in 1818. It tells the
story of Dr Frankenstein's fascination with the nature
of life itself. As an experiment he brings to life a
gigantic humanoid creature which he is unable to
control. Frank is suggesting that perhaps in Rita he has
created a monster that has developed a will of its own.

76   *Gothic*: a term used to refer to a type of literature which
emphasises the supernatural and the grotesque. Mary
Shelley's *Frankenstein* and Bram Stoker's *Dracula* are
primary examples of this.

76   *the hallmark of literature*: to guarantee quality and
authenticity, items of silver, gold or platinum are
stamped by the London Guild of Goldsmiths. Frank is
saying that Rita can now recognise genuine works of
literature.

77   *Virginia*: Virginia Woolf (1882–1941), whose novels
include *Mrs Dalloway* (1925) and *To the Lighthouse* (1927).
She was a central figure in the intellectual Bloomsbury
set.

77   *Or Charlotte? Or Jane? Or Emily?*: three famous women
writers. Charlotte Brontë (1816–55), best known for the
novel, *Jane Eyre*. Jane Austen (see note to page 20).
Emily Brontë (1818–48), sister of Charlotte and known
for her poetry and the novel, *Wuthering Heights*.

Scene Seven

78   *tea chests*: loose-leaf tea used to be shipped to the UK in
large boxes made of plywood and lined with silver foil.
Once unpacked, the chests used to make ideal packing

cases and were in common use by removal firms before the advent of plastic and cardboard containers.

79 *metaphorically*: Frank is saying that he did not literally 'bugger the bursar'. In the film version, Frank is drunk and disorderly beneath the bursar's window and wakes him up before collapsing on the lawn.

79 *Bon voyage*: French for 'Have a good journey'.

79 *Forster's Lager*: Frank is pronouncing Foster's Lager with an Australian accent. Foster's Lager is a popular Australian beer launched by the Foster brothers in 1887. However, it was not widely available in the UK until the late 70s and early 80s when it became known through advertisements starring the Australian actor and comedian, Paul Hogan. Frank is reminding Rita of her mispronunciation of E. M. Forster's name in Act One, Scene One.

Questions for Further Study

1. 'I wanted to write a play which would attract and be as valid for the Ritas in the audience as the Franks' (Willy Russell). In what ways has Willy Russell succeeded in achieving this aim?

2. The Rita at the beginning of the play is far more interesting than the Susan she insists on being towards the end. How far do you agree with this statement?

3. 'The play is just as much about educating Frank as it is about educating Rita.' Who benefits the most from the relationship in the play and why?

4. To what extent can *Educating Rita* be considered a period play?

5. How would you account for the immense popularity of *Educating Rita* with theatre audiences?

6. With only two characters on stage, there is a danger that any production of *Educating Rita* could be a very static affair. As a director of the play how would you ensure that the audience's interest is maintained throughout the performance?

7. What does the play have to say about the class system in Britain in the seventies and eighties and to what extent is the play relevant today?

8. Frank suggests in Act Two, Scene Five, of the play that like Frankenstein he has created a monster. Why does he say this and how far do you think he is responsible for the change in Rita?

9. There are a lot of laughs to be had in *Educating Rita*. Identify different moments of humour in the play and explain how Willy Russell achieves the comic effects.

10. *Educating Rita* is a popular stage play but does it have anything serious to say?

11. Like Rita's suggestion for staging Ibsen's *Peer Gynt,* the play could work equally well on the radio. What would be lost by not producing it for a live theatre audience?

12. How does Willy Russell chart the changes in Rita?

13. The play is firmly set in Liverpool and Rita's dialect and accent are essential ingredients of her character. However the play is frequently performed all over the world and its location has been altered to suit audiences. How significant is the location to the play's success in performance and what changes would you have to make in order for it to work in a different region?

14. 'There is an extraordinary imbalance in the quality of the writing. Character often makes way for an idea, but, more dangerously, an idea sometimes makes way for an unnecessary quip.' How far is this statement true of *Educating Rita?*

15. Consider the play from the point of view of the costume designer. How would you dress Rita and Frank in each scene and how would costume changes reflect the changes in their characters?

16. One of the major themes of the play is education. What does *Educating Rita* have to say about education and what do we learn from it as an audience?

17. Willy Russell says that the play is 'about somebody who had to arrive at a point in her life where she had more control over her life, more choice'. How does the play show this and how does Rita's experience afford her more choice?

18. Willy Russell describes Frank as 'a sardonic old bastard'. What does he mean by this and how true is this of the Frank as he comes across in the play?

19. The play is set in one room and the stage setting is an essential element of any successful production of the play. Given the brief description at the start of the play, how would you create the look of the room and position the necessary furniture? How might the set and lighting change during the course of the play to suggest the passage of time?

20. Willy Russell says that he wanted to write a love story. What kind of love story is *Educating Rita* and is this a useful description of the play?

STEVE LEWIS was born in Andover, Hampshire, and has studied at Middlesex, Exeter and Sussex Universities. He began his career as a Youth Theatre Director at the Everyman Theatre, Liverpool, followed by many years as a teacher in further education and director of over 100 student and community productions. He has held the positions of Qualifications Leader for Performing Arts with Edexcel and Senior Lecturer in Drama Education at the University of Central England. He is a consultant for Drama with the Qualifications and Curriculum Authority and is Director of Visual and Performing Arts at City College, Brighton and Hove. Steve has published three volumes of play collections in the Collins Short Plays Plus series, adapted Euripides' *The Trojan Women*, which has been widely used as an A-level set text, and written the commentary and notes for the Methuen Drama Student Edition of Theatre Workshop and Joan Littlewood's *Oh What A Lovely War*.